09

Writing Comedy for Television

Writing Comedy for Television

BRIAN COOKE

with cartoons by the author

METHUEN

First published in Great Britain 1983
by Methuen London Ltd
11 New Fetter Lane, London EC4P 4EE

Copyright © 1983 Brian Cooke

Printed in Great Britain
by Richard Clay (The Chaucer Press) Ltd,
Bungay, Suffolk

British Library Cataloguing in Publication data:

Cooke, Brian
    Writing comedy for television.
    1. Comedy programs   2. Television authorship
    I. Title
    808'.066791021   PN1992.7

    ISBN 0–413–51820–5
    ISBN 0–413–51830–2 Pbk

For Philip Jones OBE,
without whom this book would not have been possible . . .

Contents

Introduction

Before we get up close to the coal-face, so to speak, it might be a good idea to survey the general terrain. Television comedy writing falls into two main categories – the situation comedy and the sketch show.

A glance through two television programme guides reveals that in an average week there are eighteen sitcoms and seven sketch shows on the air. In just one week! In some other week there might well be more sketch shows but there will seldom be less sitcoms. After all, it's less than one per channel per night.

Some of these are brand-new shows, some are second, third or fourth series of established favourites, some are repeats, some are American reruns and some are golden oldies, enticingly presented as 'A fifth chance to see . . .'. They have only one thing in common. They all had to be written by somebody. Apart from that one common factor, they're all different. The diverse world of television comedy encompasses every style of writing, from the broad comedy of 'Are You Being Served?' to the often painful, gentler wit in 'Butterflies'. From the technical trickery in 'Rentaghost' to the frequently biting sketches of 'Not the Nine O'Clock News' is a long, long journey. On the way you can do an eyes-right towards the character comedy of 'It Ain't 'Arf Hot, Mum' or you can left-wheel down memory lane with Sergeant Bilko, still an object lesson in tight, well-written dialogue.

The first decision you have to make is this: which style of writing will come naturally to you? What kind of comedy show would you be happiest writing? It's a decision you don't have to make for a while. It's something you can think about when we've sorted out the differences between them all, when we've sign-posted the various paths you can follow a little more clearly.

Comedy does change direction, almost from year to year. Perhaps two decades ago the programme guides might have summed up a sitcom episode as follows: 'High jinks ensue when Wendy burns the roast joint and her husband's boss is coming to dinner!'

In theory, the audience at home would hug itself with delight at the thought of the scatterbrained housewife struggling to cope with the situation. They knew nothing serious was going to happen to the characters. They might lose their car keys or decide to stop smoking but that was about as traumatic as it would get.

Not any more. These days the programme blurb would be just as likely to read something like this: 'Wendy argues with her husband about whether he should have a vasectomy or she should continue taking the pill!'

Television comedy has grown up. Not all of it, because you'll still find Wendy burning the roast joint in certain shows. But you'll also find other shows that tackle more serious subjects, that wring laughter out of sex, or divorce, or death, and where the children aren't the little angels that they never really were, anyway. Except in sitcomland.

And the audience has grown up, too. Fifteen or twenty years ago a sketch series was usually cosy, a pleasant romp. Arthur Haynes would upset Nicholas Parsons by turning up at a regimental dinner in his tramp outfit. Or Charlie Drake would trot into the dole office, demanding his rights and having a slanging match with the man behind the counter. Remember? Well, maybe you don't, but you can take my word for it. It was fairly easy going.

Then along came 'That Was The Week That Was'. It blew a hurricane of fresh air into the sketch show format. Sketches and quickies about homosexuals, class warfare, politicians . . . anybody or anything was a target. Nothing was sacred and the audience obviously agreed. They watched. And sketch shows haven't been quite the same since. Marty Feldman, Peter Cook and Dudley Moore all seized their opportunities and helped educate the audience to its present level of awareness. Helped it grow up.

Sure, lots of today's sketch series still use pieces that might have been written in the sixties, and the audience still watches them. But the other shows are there, too. Mike Yarwood can parody the royal family. Janet Brown can satirise Margaret Thatcher. As far as television comedy is concerned, there's never been a better time to be a writer.

Thanks to the pioneering work of 'Till Death Us Do Part', 'Steptoe', 'TW3' and many others, your subject matter is infinite. You can tackle any problem, any attitude, whether in a sketch or a sitcom, and be bound by only your own good taste. And the good taste of the people who are going to buy the stuff from you. This doesn't mean you can be rude, or filthy. Being controversial was never enough for any of the shows I've mentioned. They were, and are, all very funny as well.

This, I'm afraid, is going to be a recurring theme. Whatever sketch or sitcom you eventually write has to be amusing. Even if it's beautifully written, compelling in its content and fearsome in its integrity, its prime purpose is to promote laughter. I shall keep nagging away at this basic point because it's probably the most important one in this whole book and you'd better believe it.

OK, time to do a little work. First off, I'd like to take a look at situation comedy. Those of you who want to write sketches and quickies, move to the back for a while, but pay attention. Everything that applies to sitcom applies just as much to sketches, too. More so, sometimes. We'll tackle sketches and quickies in great detail later on, but first let's examine sitcoms. You know you can write them better than some of the ones that are already on the air . . .

No wonder you can't think of anything. You're not plugged in . . .

① What is a Situation Comedy?

This isn't such a daft question as it looks at first glance. It won't do any harm to clarify in your own mind exactly what you're attempting to write.

Let's make it quite clear what you are not trying to write. You're not attempting a drama script. You want people to laugh at what you're writing. Your characters can, and should be, as fully rounded as any characters in a straight television play. But the pressure is on them to say amusing things more or less all the time.

You're not writing a serial. Each episode, especially the first one (or the 'pilot', as it's called), should be completely self-contained. There are a few exceptions to this, but let's learn the basic rules before we start breaking them. Each episode will finish with a satisfying solution to the plot that featured in it. You're telling an anecdote and you've got to pay it off rather than leave it hanging in mid-air.

You're not writing for the theatre or radio. You're not confined to one set and you don't have the luxury of unlimited imaginary locations. You haven't got the sizable budget of a feature film and you can't use a cast of thousands.

So what is a TV sitcom? It's a series of short scenes, shot in a studio in front of an audience and nowadays it will cost about fifty thousand pounds to make. That's each episode. Occasionally you can have a filmed insert, usually filmed weeks before, in order to show something that can't be done in the studio. A car smash, a train leaving a station, that sort of thing.

Each of these scenes are like the chapters of a book. They

reveal the story, bit by bit, telling the audience what you want them to know at that particular time. Occasionally you'll 'plant' something in a scene that will flower later. Mostly each scene will just push the story along, perhaps revealing a little more about the characters while you're at it.

Situation comedy characters are usually normal people involved in real life situations. Just like your Auntie Hilda and Uncle Wilf. These situations almost invariably revolve around their home or their work or both.

It's as well to limit your characters in your pilot episode. After all, the less people there are, the more time you can devote to each one, the more you can develop them. And speaking of 'time', you might as well get used to the idea of 'sitcom' time. You don't start a story and follow it through, minute by minute, as in real life. You dip into your character's day, choosing to show what you want in order to tell your story. Each scene can be hours apart if it suits you, or they can cover a period of days or weeks.

All right, that's enough lecturing for the moment. Let's do some work. Let's take a typical pilot episode of a brand-new sitcom called, for want of a better title, 'Hilda and Wilf'.

I'm not going to write the thing. At this stage we're just going to see if there's anything there. I've got a half notion. I'm now going to sit down with a stack of unlined paper and a few pencils and take a closer look at it. There's no point in launching into the writing of the hilarious first scene if I don't know what the fourth scene is going to be.

Here's my half notion. The generation gap is often at its widest when the children of a family are teenagers. Suppose we take a family with three teenage kids, all old enough to leave home. But they won't go. It's too comfortable at home, with Mum doing the cooking and washing and ironing and Dad paying for the heating and the food.

Mum doesn't mind but Dad is beginning to resent it. His home isn't his own any more. There's no privacy. Yet he can't throw his children out. Where would they go? It's his duty to provide a roof over their heads until such time as they choose to leave.

So far we're on very familiar territory. But . . . suppose, instead of the kids leaving home, the parents did?

Suppose Mum and Dad rented a small flat, leaving the three teenagers in the house to cope for themselves? Would this give us the basis for a new sitcom?

It's a simple enough idea. Let's play with it for a while. 'Hilda and Wilf' . . .

2/ Hilda and Wilf

I see Wilf as aged about forty-five. He's at the age when dissatisfaction with his life is beginning to set in. He paints with water-colours but he knows he's not very good. He feels that he's putting up with life rather than living it. He's worked at the same job for thirty years. Something must be done but he doesn't know what.

Very much a stock sitcom character.

Hilda, his wife and mother of his children, is quite happy with her lot. She asks no more than to continue with her life in exactly the same way as it's been going since she got married. She may be aware of Wilf's discontent but she doesn't share it. Another stock sitcom character.

Look, I didn't say we were going to break any new ground. I'm just showing you how a show gets started. It's quite possible that during the course of blocking out – or planning – this pilot all the above will get thrown away. Wilf may finish up as a seventy-year-old transvestite. Hilda may turn out to be a golden-hearted tart of thirty-three. I don't know.

Actually, I do know. They're going to stay much as they are. But normally, at this stage, nothing is fixed. We're exploring, probing to see if we've got anything. Building up our pilot episode story-line.

Scene one. First of all, let's establish them in their normal environment, get to know it a little. Let's set this first scene in their kitchen. It's breakfast time. It's good if this opening scene has something in it that's known in the trade as a 'cowcatcher' or a 'thirty-second boffo'. It's almost self-explanatory. Early on in your episode you do something that will grab the audience's attention. Something that will make them want to continue to view, if only in disbelief.

How about if Wilf strolls into breakfast, smoking his pipe and wearing a frilly dress? It's not exactly subtle but, as a viewer, it'd intrigue me. Especially if Hilda didn't notice at first. She continues to cook breakfast and natter on about their children. I'd hang on just to see what her reaction is when she does notice.

We'd then learn from Wilf that this is his way of making a protest. His daughter keeps borrowing his clothes, his shirts, waistcoats, ties, etc. So why can't he do the same to her? Show her how inconvenient it can be. Maybe we should meet the daughter at this point. She's a scruffy, careless teenager of about seventeen. She's wearing Wilf's shirt, waistcoat, tie. Purely for fashionable reasons and shortage of cash.

She won't have more than a quick swig of coffee because we want to keep the pace of the show going. She's on her way out to pick up her Social Security money. Can she borrow the bus fare? Let's have Hilda give it to her, showing her fond, indulgent attitude.

Already we've established a number of things. Hilda and Wilf are married. Wilf isn't exactly happy. They've got a feckless daughter. We've got some conflict going. It's probably about page three.

Let's throw in some more conflict. It's the very life-blood of this sort of comedy. Enter the two sons of the household. Exit the daughter after a small squabble with her brothers. Establish the two boys' attitude to their father. Nothing unusual, they just don't get on. It's the generation gap.

How old are the boys? Well, if they're under sixteen in real life, we can't use them on the night of the actual recording. It's not allowed by the various educational authorities. We can record their scenes in the afternoon, without an audience, then play them back on the TV monitors when the studio audience arrives. The timing of the lines will go all to pieces, though. And half of our funny dialogue will be drowned by laughter.

We don't need that kind of problem. Let's make them eighteen and twenty. We'd better have Wilf peel the dress off before people begin to wonder. And he'd better be dressed underneath, for the sake of decency.

We continue to establish the relationships of our characters. Wilf will get very little conversation from his sons. They'll both have their ears glued to their portable Japanese radios. Hilda, however, thinks the sun shines out of their Aiwas and we'll show that, too. Eventually Wilf will leave for work. His boss wants to see him. It could be that rise or the long-awaited promotion. Wilf exits. We stay with the others because we want to plant something. We mention that the boys are thinking of having a party that evening. Since they're not working, either, they'd like to borrow some cash. Hilda will oblige. End of scene one. It's page six.

There's another reason for staying with the scene after Wilf has gone. It enables Wilf to hare across the studio to the next set and be ready for the following scene. And on transmission it will give a smoother flow to the show. If we left Wilf in the kitchen, and then cut to him entering the office (our next scene), it could be a little jerky. It can be done that way but in this case we had to stay and plant the party.

Let's move on to scene two. I'm not sure what Wilf does for a living but it doesn't matter too much because he's about to lose his job. Let's say he works in the office of a cat food company. Their new line of mouse-flavoured morsels has failed. Redundancies are about to happen and Wilf is going to be out of work.

This will be a straightforward office set and we'll meet his boss. Could be a useful character here for future development in a series. He and Wilf will talk for a while and we'll get the chance to establish further problems with Wilf's kids. Mention the all-night parties, the music constantly playing. Build up that Wilf is unhappy, that his home isn't his own any more.

Let's say for the moment that the boss hasn't got any children of his own. His rosy, idealised version of what a family life must be like can contrast with Wilf's reality. Think of what we can do to make the boss a character. Perhaps he's a hypochondriac. Or a poor businessman. No need to go into too much detail at this stage.

Anyway, Wilf is out of work. He's got a tin clock and a chunk of redundancy money coming to him. Let's go back home again.

The office scene must be worth about three and a half pages so we're heading for page ten. So far we've used two sets. We've got a few in hand so we'll set this next scene in the living-room. Let's have a partly stripped motor-bike spread around, with the youngest son working on it. Hilda will bring him coffee and they'll talk. Establish here that both lads are looking for work. They're not complete and utter layabouts or the audience will dislike them too much. Perhaps a reminder of the party would be useful. A chance here to show a little of Hilda's naivety. She still thinks that her children's parties are the same as they were when they were a lot younger, with lemonade and pin-the-tail-on-the-donkey.

Bring in Wilf, home from work. Now, how does he tell his wife that he's been sacked? Don't waste the potential of this part of the scene. The audience knows something that Hilda doesn't. She was under the impression that Wilf was seeing his boss about a rise or a promotion. Her innocent questions can provoke audience laughter, considering the real circumstances.

But she'll eventually get the picture. Thirty years of working for the cat food company and now Wilf is out of work. The only breadwinner in the family is about to start loafing around. Wilf can look on the bright side. He'll have a chance to concentrate on his painting. Hilda says he can start with the kitchen. Page what . . .? Twelve? Thirteen?

Let's jump in time and place, up to the bedroom about midnight. Wilf and Hilda in bed, continuing their discussion about what the future holds. To get to this scene we'll have had a 'tape stop'. This is when the whole of the recording process will stop and the cameramen, sound men, lighting console, everybody in the studio will stop working. They can't start again until Hilda and Wilf have changed out of their day-time clothes and into pyjamas. This can take several minutes and to keep the recording tape rolling during their costume change could mean that we'd run out of tape before the end. So we all stop and wait, and the director will fidget and scowl and worry about his blood pressure.

Actually, there is one person working like a lunatic during the tape stop and that is the 'warm-up' man. We'll deal with him later. Sufficient to say that he's out there now, keeping the studio audience from cooling down and earning his fifty quid, plus expenses, per show. And getting more laughs than the show is, if you're not careful.

Hilda and Wilf are ready. They've changed, taken up their positions in the bed. We're rolling again and they're talking about paying off the mortgage on the house. It's a sizable redundancy payment. He could eke out the rest until he can find another job. At his age? He's getting depressed.

During this conversation we can hear music and laughter coming from the living-room. The party, remember? How about interrupting their discussion by having the bedroom door burst open? Two young partygoers looking for a quiet place, preferably with a bed, to discuss Kirkegaard. Wilf incensed. This party is getting out of hand. Hilda points out that the two interlopers were married. 'But not to each other . . .'

Wilf decides to check up on the situation downstairs. Page fifteen or thereabouts.

Back to the living-room. Night-time. A lively party, featuring all three of their kids and a dozen other youngsters. Unless they actually speak, the rest are rather cynically called 'noddies'. It's all happening down here, very much a male/female party, very lively. Wilf arrives, pulling on his dressing gown. He can attempt to tone the party down without having much success. We can also use the kitchen set here; the two rooms will almost certainly be linked. So, more partygoing in the kitchen.

Let's pile on the agony. Let's have the eldest son take Wilf to one side and confide that his girlfriend is moving in with him. It's not a question, it's a statement. No, they're not getting married. It's just that she doesn't get on with her parents. And she's just a teeny-weeny bit pregnant. Wilf struggles to get back to the safety of his bedroom. Page eighteen.

We're heading towards the end of part one or the commercial break. Even if it's not an ITV show, it's no bad thing to have a twist or development in your plot at this stage.

Back in the bedroom. Wilf returns, climbs in beside Hilda. He's had enough. The house isn't his own any more. (He's mentioned this before, of course.) Obviously, his children aren't going to move out, not for years. In fact, they're about to gain another one and a quarter. It's at this point that Wilf makes the momentous decision. The point we've been working towards all along.

If the kids won't move out of the house, he will! He and Hilda will rent or buy a little flat, start life all over again, leave the kids to fend for themselves. They can start paying the mortgage, cleaning up after themselves, cooking, washing. It'll be good for them. They'll have to do it one day, why not now, while Wilf is young enough to start again, too? Hilda looks stunned.

Twenty or twenty-one pages, between thirteen and fifteen minutes long. You can scribble the magic words: 'End of Part One'.

What happens in Part Two we'll never know. I told you I wasn't going to write the whole thing. Several developments might happen. He'll certainly have to move out, leaving the three teenagers to cope on their own. Whether Hilda will go with him is another matter. We might save her leaving for another episode.

The kids' reaction to his decision could be very interesting. They probably wouldn't believe it at first. They'd probably feel that they could cope if Mum and Dad left. Finding out, during the course of several shows, that they couldn't would be what the series is about.

How would Wilf manage? Sudden peace and quiet might not be all that he thought it would be. And Hilda, torn between husband and (to her) helpless children, how would she react to having a husband under her feet all day long?

Far-fetched? As a matter of fact, it's all based on one newspaper clipping. It actually happened.

The whole purpose of going into such detail is to show you how to begin to formulate your own sitcom, how to rummage around for background and character, how to twist and turn a basic notion into a workable plot, a playlet with laughs.

So, that's what a situation comedy is; a playlet with laughs. It's an aspirin tablet for a world that's suffering from chronic migraine.

He's in his room, working on a script. Hold on, I'll see if he's awake . . .

3: What's the point of doing a story line?

I know, I know. You want to get on with the enjoyable bit, the actual writing of the script. You can't wait to get on with that hilarious scene in the attic, when the wife discovers the old love letters and reads them out to her embarrassed husband.

But a story-line will help you enormously. It's basically a filleted script. You work out and write down the running order of your scenes. You explain (to yourself, mainly) what motivates the characters to do what they're doing. You plant your plot points, work out where you're going, what you need to say in each individual scene. You find out if you've *got* a script before you start writing. You even work out how long each scene will be, so as to make sure the script will be the right length, as we did in 'Hilda and Wilf'.

And it can be very encouraging when you're struggling to write a difficult setting-up scene to know that you're coming up to one that can't fail.

You wouldn't start out on a longish journey without some sort of guide or map, would you? That's exactly what your story-line is. A guide, a battle plan, a skeleton, an essential part of your script.

It will also enable you to keep track of the 'time factor'. If the whole plot takes place in one day and you've had someone post a letter and get a reply, then you'll see from your story-line that it won't work. It'll have to be two or more days. The worst thing in the world for a new writer is to have a smug director point out that you haven't done your homework. 'You said in scene one that he's only got one leg. How come he runs for a bus in scene three?'

Another useful thing about blocking out your whole show before you start scripting: you can see how many characters and sets you've got.

It's difficult to give a rule about the number of sets you can have. It depends on the size of them. If you must have the Albert Hall built in the studio then you'd better have all the action taking place there and forget about the scene in Westminster Cathedral.

Roughly speaking, you can have five normal-sized sets in any one episode. Living-rooms, bathrooms, kitchens and so forth are considered to be normal. Stairs and small hallways you can count as half a set. They all take up studio space and they all cost money.

Problems arise if you want an outdoor set in the studio. A back garden, for instance, would take up quite a lot of space, simply because the designer has to make it look real. His backcloth has to be far enough away so that the camera doesn't show the painted trees and the cardboard apples. And the lighting can be a problem. Gardens are full of shades and shadows and a studio set has to be brighter than normal, even in these days of advanced technology. Better to set the scene in a greenhouse, or even a potting shed. Or use one of your filmed inserts.

If you want a character to climb up into an attic – actually climb *up* into it – then the set will have to be raised a couple of feet. They won't a dig a hole in the studio floor. It's no problem to build up a set (at least, it's not your problem) but you might as well be aware of it.

Which is what your story-line does for you. It makes you aware of the shape of your whole show. How tightly you've plotted, where the flabby scenes are. 'This seems a dull bit. What's it doing for me? Can I cut it or lose it altogether?'

Your story-line is a halfway stage to the actual script. It can free you from worrying, even subconsciously, about where you're going. The more work you put in at this stage, the easier the next stage, the actual writing, will be.

Are you convinced? I hope so. The desk drawers of the world are full of half-written scripts because their writers didn't know where they were going and ran out of steam. Before you start writing, you'll know.

One final point. This story-line is for your benefit only. It's a waste of time to send it in to a television company. Even if it all hangs together they won't know whether you can work it up into an acceptable script. How could they? They've never heard of you. Not yet, anyway.

④ OK, but what do I write about?

Anything you fancy, is the short answer. You can try finding a Part Two for 'Hilda and Wilf', if you like. No? Please yourself.

Actually, this is a helluva question. I don't even know what you do for a living. Is there anything there? At least you'd know the background. All professional writers are used to people coming up to them, drawing them into a quiet corner and whispering the following words: 'There's a situation comedy in *my* job. The things that go on! I'd write it myself if I had the time.'

You hear this from bus-drivers, rag-and-bone-men, cartoonists, antique dealers ... and they're all absolutely right! Their jobs would make a good background for a sitcom. Only a background, though. You'll need more.

Let's take the bus-driver. Several years ago 'On the Buses' was a very successful show. It wasn't only about working on the buses. It had a whole set of interrelated characters: a driver, his conductor, the evil inspector. At home, the driver had his mother, his sister, her husband. Many of the most successful episodes hardly used the bus depot at all. The at-home characters squabbled and complained and lived out the major and minor dramas that all families have. The viewing audience could understand and sympathise. Which brings us to an interesting phrase: 'audience identification'.

'IDENTIFY: Treat (thing) as identical (with); associate oneself inseparably (with).'

The audience didn't have to make much of an effort to understand what 'On the Buses' was about. It was about people like them, characters that they could associate with themselves, or people they knew; situations that they themselves had gone through. The battle to make them laugh was half won. They felt comfortable with the series.

Incidentally, Ronnie Wolfe and Ronnie Chesney, who wrote the series, have a framed letter in their office. It was from the Head of Light Entertainment of the BBC (at the time) and it says that, in his opinion, 'On the Buses' would not work. He turned it down flat.

It ran for four years, sold all over the world and was made into three feature films. To be fair to the Head of Light Entertainment (at the time), he did pick a lot of winners, too. One BBC winner was 'Steptoe and Son', all about rag-and-bone-men.

'Ah!' you cry triumphantly, 'how many of us can identify with a junkman and his son?' True. But what we did understand was the relationship of the two characters, both dependent on each other, age versus youth, ambition versus knowledge. Simpson and Galton wrote it as a one-off pilot and weren't sure themselves that there was enough in it for a series. Only when they started to explore the characters properly did they realise what a rich seam of comedy they'd struck.

The American version ('Sandford and Son') added a further element: they were both black. But Alan Simpson says that they figured the Steptoes had enough problems without adding colour to them.

And the cartoonist? I'm cheating a little here. 'Keep It in the Family' is a series I created myself. The central character was a cartoonist, but the main premise of the series was the fact that his two daughters had moved into the vacant ground-floor flat underneath his own. So, they'd left home but they hadn't. They had the freedom but he still had the worries of knowing what they were up to, most of the time.

He also had a boss, an editor who fancied his wife. The lead character's wife, that is. So there were a number of things in the show that the viewing audience could identify with. Almost any family comedy will have ingredients in it that ring bells in the viewers' heads. That's why 'domestic' sitcoms are forever popular.

Of course, there are other sitcoms on the box, featuring policemen, astronauts, robots, almost anything you can think of. But – and think about this – the main comedy comes from the characters *relating* to each other, no matter what their job is or where they are. And it's the relationships that the audience can understand and identify with.

In the mid-sixties there was a series in America called 'My Mother, the Car'. The basic premise of the series was that the lead character's mother had died and been reincarnated as a second-hand car, a 1928 Porter Touring Mobile. Mother was able to chat to her son, through the car radio, and he bought her/it and took her/it home to his family. They resented this, because they wanted a new station-wagon and they couldn't understand why he cossetted the car so much.

I personally feel that this is asking the audience to suspend their disbelief from too high a branch. It's a weird and wonderful idea and one can only admire the creator. The point is, even in this extreme case, relationships were at the heart of the comedy.

Let's get back to your problem. You need an idea, a notion, something that will get you started, right?

The best advice I can give you sounds ridiculously simple. It's this: read the newspapers. Somewhere in every issue there's an item or an article that can be your starting point. It might even be in the small ads. That's how 'Man About the House' came into being. Johnnie Mortimer and I noticed that there were an increasing number of people advertising for 'mixed flat sharing'. Mixed? Boys and girls together? Hey, that's not been done!

We twisted it round a little, made it two girls and one boy. That was our 'weenie'.

'Weenie'? It's just a word to describe an element in a situation that makes that situation more comedic. It's the added ingredient that turns an ordinary idea into something better, gives it more potential.

We added another ingredient to the show in the shape of the downstairs landlord and landlady, George and Mildred Roper. The three kids sharing the flat had almost total freedom, no parents to worry about. So George and Mildred became surrogate parents, authority figures.

Then we gave poor George his own personal 'weenie', a very low sex drive. It's astonishing how many bells that rang. It seems there are an awful lot of frustrated Mildreds in the world. One lady in America wrote in, suggesting a line for Mildred to use about George's poor sexual performance: 'You can't push a marshmallow into a piggy bank.'

When you're rummaging around for your own situation comedy idea, bear the 'weenie' in mind. And let's not forget the 'audience identification', either.

One or two more points. Don't expect the idea for your first sitcom series to just pop into your head. It might, but it's more likely to come slowly, in bits and pieces. You'll get a vague notion, perhaps prompted by a piece in a newspaper or magazine. With a little thought this may firm up into a half idea. Work on that. Polish it. Make notes. Perhaps the thought of a particular performer playing the main character will get you excited. 'Or suppose I made it a *woman*! Aha!'

Don't fall in love with your first thoughts. Be prepared to go down a path that might be a dead end. Back yourself into a corner, see if you can figure out how you, or your characters, would react. Try several reactions. Which one will lead you furthest along your plot line? Add a scene to the early part. Take one out. Is it beginning to shape up into a story-line? No? Then lay it aside for a while, let your subconscious work on it. Start on a different idea. You'll get there, eventually. If it was easy, everybody would be doing it.

One final quote. 'Writing is easy. You just sit at your typewriter and concentrate until beads of blood form on your forehead.'

But don't get too depressed by George Axelrod's remark. Remember, you're only looking for one idea. Just one. Something that will have 'legs', and run for a while. Are you sure you don't want to try writing a Part Two for 'Hilda and Wilf'? It'd be good practice . . .

Wag your tail if you think this is funny . . .

5/ Who should I write for?

That's easy. You should write for yourself. With one eye keenly cocked on the audience at home. Not the studio audience. They're only there as a catalyst for the viewer and to keep the performers on their toes during the recording.

The studio audience is essential for these two reasons, but you must never, ever write for them or you'll fall right between every stool around. I'll repeat this, because it's important. You're writing for yourself and the viewer at home. It's between you and them, they're the ones you have to amuse. And they're usually in small groups of two or three or four. The audience laughter on the recorded show prompts the folks at home to laugh, too. People rarely laugh alone; they like a little prompting.

Funnily enough, the Americans, who started sitcoms, used to do them without a studio audience. They'd either dub on a laughtrack ('The machine *loved* the show!') or they'd play the finished tape to an invited crowd and record their laughter. These days they've copied the way we do it in England and have an audience at the actual taping. They're very pleased with themselves for doing this. They often have a credit at the end, 'Recorded in front of a live audience' (with the exception of 'MASH', which has a dubbed laughtrack on the USA version, wiped off for the British transmission).

Anyway, whichever method is used, the first person to laugh at your script has to be you. If you don't think it's funny, the odds are that nobody else will, either.

This doesn't mean that you're supposed to sit and guffaw over every sentence you write. You'll do that occasionally, of course, but most of the time you'll be coolly appraising what you've written, balancing out the funnies with the plot and character lines, keeping an eye on your time factor, wondering if you can remove any extraneous words or polish up that awkward phrase.

Which brings me to another important point. There are only three reasons why you should leave a line in a finished script. Three. No more.

1. It's funny (or a set-up for a funny).

2. It's a plot development.

3. It's a character development.

And an ideal line would do all three at once. Occasionally you'll write a line that is very funny but isn't in character. You've had someone say something because you've fallen in love with the line. Wrong. Cut it out. Or go back and change the character so that the line fits, which will probably mean losing some other good lines earlier. Better to cut. Be ruthless. Don't waste the line, though. Write it down and shove it in a file for possible future use. I've got a file full of odd jottings and out of context lines:

'It was a wonderful evening. Let's not spoil it by seeing each other again.'

'I hate to leave but I've only got ten minutes left on my twelve-hour cold capsule.'

'Maybe it's not a cold. Maybe you're allergic to Kleenex.'

'I religiously avoid talking about God.'

'Llanfairpwllgwyngyllgogerychwyrndrobwll-llantysiliogogo-goch.'

'He's got a face like a twisted plimsoll.'

'I think I've just sprained my imagination.'

I knew they'd be useful one day. I've just filled a bit of this book with them.

'Who should I write for?' is actually two questions. You may have meant to ask whether there was a particular actor or actress that you should bear in mind whilst writing. Well, why not? You're trying to make your characters real and it will certainly help if you imagine a particular performer saying the words.

You may not get John Cleese but when Ronnie Corbett accepts the part he'll benefit from the effort you put in to make the character consistent. You may have to change the height jokes, mind.

Writers can sometimes find themselves writing to please a director/producer or even a star. Let's face it, in the early stages of a writing career you'd write to please the doorman's dog if you thought it would help sell the script.

But, initially, *you* have to be happy with what you're doing. You have to write to please yourself. I'll rummage in my file and steal a pertinent quote.

'There is no formula for success, but there is a formula for failure and that is to try to please everybody.'

I'll phone the zoo! For God's sake keep writing!

6: Where do jokes Come from?

Ideally, out of the situations you've created. After all, it is called 'situation' comedy, and if you can't get laughs out of the situations you've created you've done your job wrongly somewhere along the way.

However, situations take time to build, and while you're heading towards the funny bit you've carefully set up, you need to keep your audience entertained. The dialogue has to be consistently amusing. You can't have great chunks of boring script in between your hilarious set-piece scenes and plot twists. You can't have a caption card flashed up that reads, 'Hold on, folks, there's a good bit coming in two minutes!' They won't be there to read it. They'll be playing mah-jong or they'll be out at the pub. Or – the ultimate shame for a comedy writer – they'll have switched over to 'Panorama' or 'World in Action'.

You've got to stop the audience at home from losing interest. Let's accept one thing right away. It's going to be impossible to keep them laughing out loud for half an hour. You'll force a chuckle or two out of them, maybe even a few guffaws, but most of the time your viewers will be just sitting there, smiling appreciatively. You've got to give them something to smile at, all the time.

The average script will be forty pages long, about nine speeches on each page, a total of three hundred and sixty pieces of dialogue. And every single one has to be working for you, has to earn its place in your finished script.

We've really reached the crunch-point now, because making

your dialogue crackle along in a satisfying way, without showing the strain, is not easy.

Imagine your script is a piece of music. You're orchestrating it. Your musical instruments are your characters. The drive, pace, rhythm of the show will be dictated by your words.

I'm not going to stretch this analogy any further, but I do think it's a fair one. The dictionary definition of 'rhythm' speaks of a 'measured flow of words . . . the harmonious correlation of parts, movement with regulated succession of strong and weak elements or of opposite or different conditions.'

That's exactly what your script should be, with one added element. It's got to be funny, too.

Years ago, when Frank Muir and Denis Norden worked for the BBC, they met Mel Brooks. He asked them what they did at the Beeb and they proudly said they were 'comedy advisors'. Mel staggered back, awed. 'You mean . . . you *know*?' he said.

Johnnie Mortimer and I wrote our first television script at about that time, having done hundreds of radio shows. I remember Frank dropping in to the rehearsal room. We were struggling to rewrite a page that featured a middle-aged lecher chatting up a young girl. Frank glanced at the script and suggested a line for him: 'Let me put another colour in your paint-box . . .'

It fitted nicely and we thanked him. 'It's only a one-liner,' he said, drifting away in a cloud of pipe smoke.

After several years as a comedy advisor myself, I've discovered that the 'one-liner' is only one of a number of basic approaches to dialogue. Analysing comedy is like shovelling smoke, but I'll try. Remember, these are only basics, but if you find yourself wondering how to tackle a tricky scene, try applying one of these approaches.

1 The misunderstanding

This is where you have one character, deliberately or otherwise, misunderstand something that's been said. From 'George and Mildred', in a scene where George is holding up a glass of his somewhat cloudy home-brewed beer:

MILDRED (SUSPICIOUS). It's got funny little things, swimming about in it.
GEORGE. They're hops!
MILDRED. All right, they're hopping about in it!

Or Patrick Glover, in 'Father, Dear Father', is looking for a flat for his daughter. He's complaining to an estate agent:

PATRICK. We've been to Hampstead, Chalk Farm, Camden. We've driven all over the place . . . nothing.
AGENT. Have you tried Tooting?
PATRICK (BAFFLED). D'you think it would help?

I have to confess that these examples, taken out of context, do look a bit feeble. Still, as part of a scene, they both worked. The misunderstanding often hinges on one key word. Done properly, it's the unexpectedness of it that prompts laughter.

2 Cross-purpose talking
An extension of the above, where you sustain the misunderstanding for more than one or two speeches. Basically, it's two or more characters thinking they're all talking about the same thing, but they're not. They're talking at cross-purposes. Obviously, it has to be set up, but once you've done that every line should get its reaction.

From 'Keep It in the Family', a scene in a bedroom where a young artist has been mistaken for the expected decorator. He feels that there's something vaguely sexy about to happen. Muriel simply wants her bedroom decorated properly. Dudley did it last time and made a poor job of it.

DUDLEY (INTRODUCTIONS). This is my wife. Muriel, Andrew. He's the painter.
MURIEL (BRISKLY MAKING BED). Oh, yes. Good. Hullo.
DUDLEY. D'you know . . . and I'm ashamed of this . . . it's three years since we did it last? (*TO* MURIEL) Isn't it?

MURIEL. Nearly four.

ANDREW. That's . . . uh . . . that's a l . . . long time.

MURIEL. He wanted to do it again but I wouldn't let him.

ANDREW. Ah, well . . .

MURIEL. He made such a mess of the ceiling last time. And the wallpaper.

DUDLEY. I happen to like it upside down.

MURIEL. Well, I don't. I want it done properly. (*TO* ANDREW) Let's get a man in, I said.

ANDREW. It's very kind of you, but . . .

MURIEL. He didn't even do the bit behind the wardrobe.

ANDREW. What bit behind the –? I don't think you should be telling me this . . .

DUDLEY. I'll leave you to it. She'll explain what she wants. Needs to be completely stripped.

And Dudley prepares to exit but the young man beats him to the door, leaving Muriel (and indeed Dudley) completely baffled.

The danger with cross-purpose talking is that you'll be tempted to carry it on for too long. Resist the temptation. Better to leave your audience wanting more than to strain the credibility of your characters.

3 *The one-liner*

Now this is where you really do have to work. Flashes of inspiration are allowed. The one-liner comes in many forms, all of which will give that extra edge to your script. It's the closest thing to a deliberate joke that you'll write.

It's often a way of getting over information in an amusing way. Instead of a character saying, 'It's raining,' he could say, 'Strewth! I reckon the angels were on the beer last night.'

Or, instead of saying 'I'm in trouble,' he'd say, 'I'm up that well-known creek without a roll o' toilet paper!'

The one-liners are the grace notes in the orchestration of your script, your chance to be witty, or dry or laconic or sour. Sometimes they'll be a straightforward insult. Rather than write, 'God! She's ugly!' say, 'She can turn bathtaps on and off by scowling at them!'

Even taken out of context they should stand up.

'Dad keeps using four letter words to me . . . like "find work".'

'You know your trouble . . . you suffer from delusions of adequacy.'

'Why does sliced apple always go rusty?'

I think I can best sum up by saying that if you have to get something over in your script, whether it's a plot point, a character delineation or just an exit, don't do it with a cliché. Think about it and try to turn it into a one-liner. Try to add a grace note.

4 The running gag

It's impossible to give detailed examples of the running gag without printing a complete script.

It's a joke that you start in an early scene, carry on in subsequent scenes, then pay off somewhere towards the end. It's a way of adding interest. It's a trace element that runs through your whole script or sometimes a whole series.

An example of this was George's sexual inadequacy in the 'G & M' series. Having established this, we only had to have him use an inadvertent phrase, such as, 'I haven't got the proper equipment, Mildred,' to have the audience literally waiting for the come-back. Often a look was all that was needed.

Sometimes you find yourself with a running gag that is so strong that it turns into a sub-plot. On one episode of the same series we had the little boy next door caught smoking a sneaky cigarette in the toolshed. His father decided that he was setting a bad example and decided to give up smoking himself. The running gag was his attempts to find a substitute . . . mint humbugs, toffee whirls, knitting. The pay-off came when he finally weakened and sneaked off to the toolshed for a quick drag. And the little boy found him . . .

In 'Robin's Nest' our 'runner' was a character, Albert Riddle, the one-armed Irish dishwasher. If we found ourselves with a scene that was flagging, we'd have him launch into one of his interminable tales.

> ALBERT. Y'know, that table reminds me of me Auntie Bridie. Her legs used to fold up, as well. Especially when she'd had a few drinks. Very fond of the drink, me Auntie Bridie . . . Came home one night and claimed she'd been assaulted by the village pump. Which was highly unlikely, for she was not a good lookin' woman. Mind you, though, the well did run dry for a day or two . . .

He'd ramble on with the same tale over several scenes, while we quietly got on with the plot.

The running gag is very useful indeed, and if you get more than one going, so much the better.

5 *The frustration routine*

Where one character is in a hurry and another character is being pedantic. The humour comes from the contrast between the two.

From 'Let There Be Love': the main character, Timothy Love, is trapped in a lift. He's talking on the lift telephone to the hall porter of the block of flats, who is safe in his cubbyhole.

> TIMOTHY (TO PHONE, ANNOYED). The lift is stuck between floors!
> PORTER (TO PHONE). Again? Oh, well, you'll have to use the stairs.
> TIMOTHY. I am *in* the lift.
> PORTER. Oh, well, now . . . yes. Problem there. Perhaps I should phone the engineers. What d'you think?
> TIMOTHY. Brilliant!
> PORTER. Thank you. I do m'best.
> TIMOTHY. And phone Hampstead registry office.
> PORTER. I don't think they'd know anything about lifts.
> TIMOTHY. No, no, no. I'm getting married in fifteen minutes.

PORTER. Congratulations.

TIMOTHY. Thank you. Give them a message . . . from Timothy Love. Now, write this down. 'I may be delayed, but I will be there.'

PORTER. Just a minute . . . er . . . have you got a pencil?

I have to add that he got the message wrong and that Timothy had his claustrophobic friend stuck in the lift with him. 'We're all going to die, Timothy . . .'

I'm in danger here of getting this analysis of dialogue mixed up with the situations that have been created. However, I can use the above as an example of lines that, in themselves, aren't all that funny. It's the frustration and the actual situation that make them work.

The 'frustration routine' doesn't have to be a whole set-piece scene. You can throw it in quite arbitrarily if you have a character given to whimsy. Dudley, from 'Keep It in the Family', answering the telephone in an impish mood:

DUDLEY. Hullo. This is a recorded announcement. If you wish to leave your name, do so at the third beep. Beep! Beep! Beep!

CALLER. Good morni . . .

DUDLEY. If you wish to leave a message as well as your name, wait until your hear a further beep.

CALLER. I'd just like to . . .

DUDLEY. However, if you wish to leave neither a name nor a message, ignore the previous announcement and listen for the buzz.

CALLER. I simply . . .

DUDLEY. This buzz will be followed by a five-second pause, two burps, one belch and a noise which can best be described as a big, juicy . . .

And at that point his wife snatches the telephone from him and takes over. Everybody knows what the next word is going to

be, but there is no way you can say it on TV. Which neatly
brings me to another category . . .

6 Innuendo

Or, the mucky bits. It's a great temptation for the new writer to
try to be daring and controversial, to try to get away with risqué
or downright rude dialogue, working on the assumption that
'Nobody's doing it. I'll be the first!'

Not so. There are a lot of people writing it. The reason you
don't see it on TV is because they're not selling it. I know that
most sitcoms have a dash of innuendo in them, but that's all. It's
the seasoning, not the meat and potatoes. So use it sparingly.

7 The visual

Self-explanatory, really, but worth a mention. You're writing for
television, not radio, and a little visual humour won't come
amiss.

It doesn't need to be a big, banana skin routine. It's more
useful when used *with* your dialogue.

Classic examples: someone about to squirt soda into his whisky.
He's told something he doesn't like. His reaction is to squirt too
hard involuntarily and flood his drink, splashing it everywhere.

The nervous interviewee, lighting the wrong end of a filter tip
cigarette, inhaling deeply, unaware of it. Delayed reaction here is
often funnier than an instant fit of coughing.

The equally nervous telephone caller, agitatedly fiddling with
the speaker end of his telephone, causing it to come apart in his
hands, even as he talks.

The point is, if you want this visual humour, write it in your
script. Don't rely on the actor or director to think of it for you.
Oh, and keep it simple.

8 The exaggeration

Or 'the flight of imagination', where a character, instead of saying
'I've got flu' decides to embellish it.

PATRICK. I've got Asian flu. Think of it . . . all those

oriental germs, galloping across the mountains, urging their shaggy little ponies across the seas, along the M4, down the High Street, through the letterbox and straight up my nose . . . a-a-atchoo!

It doesn't have to be as elaborate as this. In fact, the exaggeration is a close cousin to the one-liner. From 'Robin's Nest', our dishwasher is faced with a new trout tank in the restaurant.

ALBERT. Ah, will ye look at that! A bit of river in a box!

Or from 'KIITF', Dudley is complaining about his wife.

DUDLEY. I should never have rescued her from that brothel in Marseilles. Being pawed by a big, brawny Lascar, she was . . . with one eye. Called Pierre. I dunno what his other eye was called. 'Unhand that woman,' I said. I was only there to read the gas meter.
MURIEL. Sometimes I fear for your sanity.
DUDLEY. He flung a bible straight at my heart . . . but, luckily, it was deflected by a bullet in my pocket, sold to me by my granny on her deathbed . . .

See what I mean by 'flight of imagination'? Actually, that's what this whole section is about. Using your imagination to put variety into your dialogue. It's not enough to write a set-up line, followed by the pay-off line. It gets rather boring and it's also damned hard to do.

This list of approaches to dialogue is by no means complete. I could spend the rest of this book dividing and sub-dividing categories of humour. We'd both go out of our minds.

Study the sitcoms on television. Watch how the writers develop their scenes, twist and turn the words around. A lot of it is pure technique. You can learn it. You can start inventing some of your own. You can start writing . . .

⑦ A short pause for a breather

The odds are that you're going to sit down and read this book in one sitting.

I've spent the whole time up until now nagging you to think. About your basic idea, your characters, storyline and dialogue.

I have to assume that you haven't got a solid idea yet, because, as I said, you're reading this at one go. It's only when you've read it all that you're going to sit down, nostrils flaring, start scribbling like a lunatic and put me out of work.

Up until now we've been dealing with the creative side of writing situation comedy. Later on we'll get to the creative writing of sketches and quickies, but right now I'd like to take a look at some of the more practical aspects. Whether you intend to write sitcoms or sketches, the script layout will be much the same. So will the jargon used. You'll meet the same people and you'll have to sell your script in much the same way. You would-be sketch writers at the back should inch forward a bit. Most of this next section applies to you, too.

Another interesting feature about it is that you can't afford it!

8 - How do I lay out my script?

No problem. The standard layout of all light entertainment scripts is roughly the same. It varies a little from company to company, but not enough to worry about.

Before we actually get down to the layout, let me make one further point. I've always found it easier to write out the whole script in longhand. It's something to do with the permanent look that a typed line has. I'm more reluctant to change it if it looks neat and tidy. So, I do the lot in scribbly handwriting, full of crossing out and added bits on the side. Then I type it, fine editing as I go. In the long run it's just as fast as typing straight on to the page as you make it up. Try it, but if it doesn't suit you, do it whichever way you feel best.

And speaking of speed, I've found that the average time it takes me to write a half-hour script, with or without a partner, is about two and a half weeks. Comparing notes with other professional writers, I've found that they take two and a half weeks, too. If you find that you can do it in a week or less you're either a genius or you're not trying hard enough to keep up a standard.

By the way, it's a waste of time to send in a handwritten script. It won't stand a chance. Most television companies put up with unsolicited material rather than welcome it. The least you can do is make it easy for the reader. So you're going to type it, using a black ribbon only and double-spacing the whole thing.

You'll use white paper, A4 size and you'll buy the top copy paper called bond, not the flimsy stuff called bank. You'll type on one side of the paper only and you'll always, always keep one copy of the finished script for your files. This means using a carbon or running the whole thing off on a copying machine. Better to copy it, because you're probably not an expert typist and fiddling around with White-out and carbons is a messy business.

First, the title page. Let's use one of my own shows as an example. The title of the show is in the middle of the page, in capital letters: 'KEEP IT IN THE FAMILY'.

Underneath the title, in lower-case letters, is the series and episode number. In this case it'll be 'Second Series: Episode Three'. In your own case it should read 'First Series: Episode One'. There's nothing like a bit of optimism.

Underneath that you can put an episode title, also in lower-case letters. 'The Judas Goat'. And underneath that 'written by', followed by the name of the author.

That's all you need on the title page. Nothing about 'Copyright reserved' or a resumé of the plot. It is very unlikely indeed that anyone would steal your idea, but if you are really worried there is one thing you can do. Send another copy of your script, recorded delivery, to the Writers' Guild. Their address is at the back of this book. Attach a covering letter, explaining what's inside. They'll put the sealed envelope in their safe, ready to bring it out as Exhibit A at the appropriate moment. Of course, you'll have to join the Guild to avail yourself of this service. But myself, I think you're being paranoic.

After the title page comes the scene breakdown. This is simply a list of your characters and your sets. It will read something like this:

<u>CHARACTERS</u> (Speaking):

DUDLEY
MURIEL
DUNCAN
TELEPHONIST
JACQUI

<u>CHARACTERS</u> (Non-speaking):

PEOPLE AT PARTY

SETS:

BEDROOM
DUNCAN'S OFFICE
SWITCHBOARD
LIVING-ROOM

If you've written any filmed inserts, you'll list them, too. Strictly speaking, this scene breakdown isn't needed. But if you don't do it, someone else will have to, usually the production assistant to the programme, who has enough to do without listing characters and sets. So type your breakdown and right away your script has got a professional look about it.

Which brings us to the first page of the actual script. The easiest way of showing you the layout is to reproduce a few pages from 'KIITF', then explain what the various things mean afterwards.

Unlike previous examples from scripts, this time we'll do it properly. You'll notice that only the right-hand side of the page is used. Set your tabulator so that the dialogue is aligned, that is, leaving a gap between the end of each character's name and the dialogue that the character is saying.

The reason for only using half the page on a TV script is simple. It's so that the director can write a camera script on the other half.

The director writes a script? Well, no, not really. Only a camera script, which is a different thing. It indicates to the cameramen (all four of them) which parts of the action their particular camera should cover. Don't worry about it. It's what he's paid for. You've got your own problems without trying to do that job, too.

So, page one . . .

OPENING TITLES AND CRE-
DITS.

1. INT: BEDROOM: DAY:

DAY ONE. ABOUT NINE A.M.

ACCORDING TO THE MICKEY MOUSE BEDSIDE CLOCK NEXT TO THE TELEPHONE ON DUDLEY'S BEDSIDE TABLE. DUDLEY AND MURIEL ASLEEP.

THE TELEPHONE RINGS. DUDLEY SLEEPILY REACHES OUT, FUMBLES WITH THE CLOCK. THE TELEPHONE CONTINUES TO RING.

HE SITS, PICKS UP THE CLOCK, SHAKES IT IRRITABLY, STILL HALF ASLEEP.

DUDLEY. Quiet, you stupid mouse!

MURIEL. (SLEEPILY.) It's the telephone.

DUDLEY. Is it? Oh. (HOLDS CLOCK TO EAR.) Hullo?

MURIEL. (INDICATES IT.) There!

DUDLEY. Oh, yes. (PICKS UP PHONE.) Hullo?

DUNCAN. (DISTORT.) Good morning.

DUDLEY. Yes. Good morning. You have reached Dial-a-Pervert ... (HEAVY BREATHING FOR A MOMENT OR TWO.)

2.   INT: DUNCAN'S OFFICE: DAY:

DUNCAN LISTENING TO THE HEAVY BREATHING ON THE TELEPHONE, SURPRISED. HE'S AT HIS DESK, IN SHIRT-SLEEVES. WE CUT BETWEEN THEM WHERE APPROPRIATE.

DUDLEY. ... please leave your name, phone number and a short, obscene message and I'll follow you anywhere. Speak now ... beep! Beep! Beep!

DUDLEY HANDS THE PHONE TO MURIEL AND SINKS BACK ON THE PILLOW.

DUNCAN. You're a day late with your drawings again, Dudley.

MURIEL. Ah, yes. Hullo, Duncan. He's ... er ... he's just finishing it off, honestly. He's hard at work, sitting at his drawing board. (COVERS PHONE.) Make a noise like a drawing board!

DUDLEY. (SQUEAKY VOICE.) Pieces of eight! Pieces of eight!

MURIEL. What?

DUDLEY. It's got a parrot sitting on the corner.

MURIEL. Tch! (TO PHONE.) If you're passing this afternoon, you could pick it up. I'll have home-made iced buns.

DUNCAN. Ah, for one of your home-made iced buns, I'd slide down a hundred-foot razorblade.

MURIEL WINCES AT THE THOUGHT.

MURIEL. Yes, well, about four o'clock, then?

DUNCAN. I'll be there. Oh, and Muriel . . .

MURIEL. Yes?

DUNCAN. . . . tell him to get his lazy backside out of that bed!

You'll now have to flick back to each page as I make a few points. The first line 'OPENING TITLES AND CREDITS' refers to the opening part of the show where the actual title comes up on the screen, along with whoever is starring in it. In a series, it's usually the same piece of tape or film every week. On a new show, nobody knows what it will be but there will certainly be something before the episode proper begins. You and the director will probably discuss it at a later date. In the meantime, you're indicating that you know all about it.

'1. INT: BEDROOM: DAY:' gets over quite a lot of information. The number is the scene number, useful in discussions, when you want to pinpoint a place in the script. The rest of the scene heading tells us that we're in the interior (in the studio) of a bedroom and it's daytime. The 'DAY' is an instruction to the lighting people. There are only two such instructions ever used.

The other one, not surprisingly, is 'NIGHT'. You never put
'DUSK' or 'TWO MINUTES PAST THE WITCHING
HOUR' in your scene headings. You can put that sort of information in the next part, the scene setting section, if you really
feel it's needed.

'DAY ONE' is partly for the benefit of the wardrobe department. You're telling them that there may be a 'DAY TWO'
coming up later, that there may be a costume change. It's also a
way for you, and everybody else, to keep track of the 'sitcom
time' element. Until you *do* put a 'DAY TWO', everyone will
assume that it's the same day right through the script. 'DAY
TWO', by the way, doesn't mean the following day. It might do,
but it could just as easily be a week later. It's just another day.

Finally, we get to the opening line. You'll see that the character's name is in capital letters. No special reason. It's just easier
to read. As a matter of fact, everything should be in upper-case
letters except the dialogue.

You'll notice that I've occasionally put an instruction before a
speech, indicating how I feel the line should be said. This is OK,
so long as you don't do it on every single line. Actors and actresses
get very stroppy if they feel you're underestimating their intel-
ligence.

Other instructions, before or inside the dialogue, are sometimes
needed. '(PICKS UP PHONE.)', for instance. If they're needed,
fine. But, again, don't write them unless you feel they're necessary. Keep them simple. Put them in brackets to avoid having
them read out as dialogue. It's all common sense, really.

You'll notice one instruction that says '(DISTORT)', just
before Duncan's first speech. This indicates two things. One, I
didn't want to see him on the screen at that point. Two, his voice
should be distorted, since it's coming from the telephone. The
director may disagree and want to cut to Duncan. That's up to
him. I've indicated what I thought was best.

The reason I thought it was best is this: it's funnier to see his
face for the first time when he's listening to the heavy breathing
coming from the phone. That's my 'cowcatcher'. It's not a very
big one but it's all I've got.

We're on to scene two now. There is no need to worry about whether it's a 'dissolve' or a 'cut' or a 'mix'. That's the director's decision. The phrase 'WE CUT BETWEEN THEM WHERE APPROPRIATE' is a useful phrase to use on any telephone conversation. It saves you writing several scene headings, one for each end of each speech of the conversation. And you need not use '(DISTORT)' again, unless you want to make the same point as last time.

That's really all you need to know about script layout. Don't get hung up on it. So long as you get across what you want, nobody is going to worry too much about the occasional spelling error or grammatical boo-boo.

Number each page and each scene. Indicate where you think the commercial break will come by typing 'END OF PART ONE' followed by 'PART TWO'. If you send it to the BBC, retype that particular page.

Finally, you get to the end. All you need then are the words 'CLOSING CREDITS AND MUSIC OUT'.

Now comes the hard bit. You've got to sell it . . .

It's worth a try, Ethel . . .

9/ Some hard facts about Selling

Let's assume right away that you haven't got a literary agent. This isn't much of an assumption because very few new writers will have. Agents tend to approach writers, rather than the other way round. They'll only approach you if they think you've got a future and you'll only have a future if you sell something. Which is where we came in . . .

If you feel incomplete without an agent, buy or borrow the *Writers' and Artists' Yearbook*. It contains a list of literary agents. Pick one. Make sure he or she handles TV scripts, rather than books or theatre plays, and send in your script.

It's certain that the agent will know more about the current market requirements than you do. However, the chances are that he will have several scriptwriters on his books already. If he's any good, he certainly will have. He may not want, or need, another comedy writer. If he doesn't, he'll politely tell you so. You may be lucky. He may love your script and know exactly the right company to send it to. They'll buy it and you needn't bother to read the rest of this chapter.

At this stage in your writing career, you don't really need an agent. Even if you did, I doubt whether you'll get one to take you on. If you can, good for you. If you can't, read on.

There are about eight markets in the United Kingdom. That is to say, there are eight television companies that make situation comedies regularly. Eight markets doesn't sound too good, but remember, each market makes several series every single year.

First of all, let's take ITV One, the Independent Television Network.

There are fifteen ITV companies, all contributing to this network. Each company is responsible for, and covers, its own area of the country, with the exception of London. The London area has two companies looking after it, one for weekdays and one for weekends.

Each individual company makes its own programmes and tries to sell them to the others. After a lot of mostly amicable haggling and horse-trading, they finish up with a mixture of everybody's programmes, and this is ITV One.

Unfortunately, of the fifteen companies only five make situation comedies with any regularity: Thames, London Weekend Television, Granada, Yorkshire, and Central Independent Television.

Their full addresses and the areas they cover are listed in *Television and Radio*, formerly called *The Independent Broadcasting Authority Guide to Broadcasting*, along with all sorts of other information about ITV programming. It's available from the IBA whose address is at the back of this book. Alternatively, if you don't want to buy another book, you can get a free folder containing all the addresses. It's called *Who Does What on ITV* and is obtainable from the Information Office of the IBA.

Of the remaining ten ITV companies, eight never make sitcoms, mainly because of the cost and the lack of studio facilities. The other two, Anglia and Tyne Tees Television, have a record of making network drama and documentaries but rarely venture into sitcoms. However, if they got the right script, perhaps with a local flavour to it, they might just bite. Especially Anglia. If you live in either of these two areas, it might be worthwhile checking out their requirements before you start writing.

Then we have the two BBC networks. They are networks because not all the programming is made in the main television centre at Wood Lane, London. They have no less than eight English regions and three substantial production centres in Birmingham, Bristol and Manchester. And, of course, they have BBC Scotland, BBC Wales and BBC Northern Ireland.

Unfortunately, this isn't as good as it sounds. BBC Scotland have occasionally ventured into sitcoms and sketch shows, notably on New Year's Eve. But BBC Wales and BBC Northern Ireland rarely, if ever, attempt a sitcom and only occasionally do a variety show. Like the eight English regions, they supply a service for the national news bulletins and they provide material for current affairs programmes, such as 'Nationwide'. They also do their own regional news/documentaries/features, none of which is of any use to you. The BBC suggests that if you have a script of specific local interest, you should send it to the appropriate regional office.

The three substantial production centres do produce a considerable number of programmes for the BBC networks. 'All Creatures Great and Small', for instance, was a successful sitcom that was made in Birmingham. But the BBC suggests that, apart from scripts of specific local interest, you should send your material to the Head of Television Script Unit, BBC Television Centre in London (the address is at the back of this book). And you should enclose a stamped, addressed envelope. Notes on current requirements are also obtainable from the same address on request.

For further information, they publish a guide for writers called, succinctly enough, *Writing for the BBC*. It'll cost you about £1, or £1.50, including postage, and is available from the various BBC Information Offices or from BBC Publications. Check the current price by phoning the Information Office. Their address and phone number should be in your directory.

I know this book is all about writing for television but I cannot ignore the fact that BBC Radio is a keen buyer of comedy material. If you fancy having a crack at radio comedy (and almost all of today's top comedy writers started on radio), then you should address your script to the Script Editor, Light Entertainment (Radio), whose address is also at the back of the book. They say that decisions can only be made on receipt of complete, typed scripts, but that advice can be offered on detailed storylines, with sample dialogue.

Obviously, a radio comedy show will cost a lot less to make than the equivalent television show. You'll realise why it's so much cheaper when they pay you, but it is a unique training-ground for the comedy writer. Don't ignore it.

Back to television and Channel Four, the second ITV channel. Channel Four is a national network intended to complement the other ITV channel. Which means that it does carry some sitcoms and variety shows.

But it doesn't actually make any programmes, apart from presentation programmes and the weekly viewer response programme. So who makes the programmes that they're showing? Well, anybody with the right idea at the right price, is what they say. Channel Four will buy programmes from all sources for cash. And they'll put up most, if not all, of the money.

Since you're a writer and not an independent production company, this doesn't get you very far. It's possible that they may pass your script on to some independent producer who is looking for a property, but I wouldn't count on it. If you fancy trying them, the person to send your script to is the Commissioning Editor, Light Entertainment, at Channel Four.

And that's about it in the UK. Whichever company you decide to send your script to, I suggest you address it to the Head of Light Entertainment, by name, if possible. He won't read it, of course, but he'll pass it on to someone who will. You'll probably get a postcard acknowledgement of the arrival of your script. This will be followed by a longish wait of up to six weeks. Be patient. After that period, it's worth a follow-up phone call or letter.

The alternative is to address your script to a specific producer/director. Make sure you're sending it to the right company, though. Some directors move around more than others and scripts can take time to catch up with them. Directors aren't too crazy about reading unsolicited scripts, but if it's addressed to them personally they usually will.

Your covering letter should be brief. Nobody's interested in the fact that you're a dustman or that you've written several articles for the *Muckspreaders and Dirtshifters Gazette*. It's a good idea to put your name and address on the last page of your script, just in case your covering letter gets separated from it.

Let's consider the awful possibility that your script will be rejected. Don't get depressed. It's possible that you've picked a bad time. That particular company may have enough sitcoms on its plate. That particular producer/director may be too busy to read the script properly, or he may be going through a bad patch in his personal life and doesn't find anything funny.

Send it out again to another company. Persevere. Let me remind you of what President Calvin Coolidge said:

> Nothing in the world can take the place of persistence. Talent will not; nothing is more common than unsuccessful men with talent. Genius will not; unrewarded genius is almost a proverb. Education will not; the world is full of educated derelicts. Persistence and determination are omnipotent.

I'd like to emphasise one thing. If your script is any good, you'll get a reaction. All television companies really are on the lookout for new talent, especially writing talent. There is room in the UK for another twenty comedy writers, believe me.

Of course it's a competitive business, and the reason for that is simple. It pays very well indeed.

(10) Lollipop time

'Nobody but a blockhead writes for anything but money.'

SAMUEL JOHNSON

Well, OK. Who am I to argue with him? But it can also give you a lot of pleasure to work on your script, solve the problems, feel it take a satisfying shape. And it's a very gratifying feeling to see a good actor saying your words, to hear the studio audience falling about at things you've created, to know that a show you wrote is *working*.

However, let's talk about the money you'll get when you sell your pilot script and any subsequent scripts.

If you've sold it to any of the ITV companies you can't be paid less than one thousand, five hundred and fifty-three pounds per episode. That's for a brand-new writer to television, who hasn't had a single thing on the box in his life. Even if you're not a member of the Writers' Guild, the Guild won't let them pay you a penny less. At the time of writing that is the minimum fee agreed by the Guild and all the ITV companies.

The maximum fee for an established writer is way, way above that. It's not uncommon for a successful comedy writer to get four and a half thousand pounds for a half-hour script. (Actually, on ITV, it's only twenty-four minutes and thirty seconds. The rest is commercials.)

You're also entitled to a fifty-pound expenses fee, twenty-five pounds for attending the read-through and twenty-five for being at any one rehearsal, or even the actual show. You won't get these expenses unless you're a member of the Writers Guild.

Join as soon as you've sold a script. Their address is at the back of this book.

If your pilot or series is repeated you'll get the same amount all over again! A one hundred per cent repeat fee, even if it's only repeated in one of the fifteen ITV regions. If it's repeated later in another one, you don't get paid again. Let's not be greedy.

That's only the beginning. Let's assume you've got a series going that isn't a flop. It's successful. There are lots of countries in the world that also have television time to fill. It's cheaper to buy an English show than to make one themselves. They'll almost certainly want to buy your series. You'll get another cheque from them, a percentage based on your original fee.

You don't have to do anything. All the ITV companies have people buzzing around the world with their briefcases stuffed full of taped TV shows, trying to sell them. 'Father, Dear Father' has been sold to thirty-four different countries at the time of writing, and every single one paid the writers a fee.

The percentages vary from country to country. Spain, for instance, only pay a miserable four per cent. The tapes are dubbed, of course. I've seen 'George and Mildred' squabbling in fluent Spanish, and all the 'Robin's Nest' team gabbling in perfect Italian. When the actors concerned visit these countries the locals are often bitterly disappointed that they only speak English. Italy pays twelve and a half per cent, by the way.

Australia pays twenty-two and a half per cent and buys almost everything. Even Sweden pays ten per cent. Western Germany pays sixty per cent, but doesn't buy a great deal. If your shows were sold to any of the three major networks in the USA, you'd get two hundred per cent. Twice as much as you got in the first place! But don't hold your breath while you're waiting; the networks have never bought the tapes of any English series. On the other hand, maybe they'll start with yours . . .

All these fees and residual percentages also apply to scripts sold to the BBC. Perhaps the initial fees are a little lower, but not much. And, with the BBC, you've always got the possibility that they'll do a second repeat on BBC Two. Two repeat fees! The same applies to Channel Four, or ITV Two.

So, it's not impossible, if your overseas percentages add up, to be paid four times for the same script. There must be a great temptation at this point to fling this book aside and rush to your typewriter. Don't do it. I haven't finished yet.

Video cassette recordings have been and are being made of many popular comedy series. These, too, are sold worldwide. It's a small market, as yet, but it's growing and it pays all over again.

Then there are the other spin-offs, such as films, stage versions of a series, books based on the scripts, games, puzzles and cartoon strips.

The radio rights are often very profitable, too. Not just in England, which tends to use only BBC shows. In South Africa, for instance, Equity, the actors' union, has stopped the sale of TV tapes for reasons of apartheid. But you can't segregate a radio audience and almost every TV series I've ever written has had a radio version put out in South Africa. Old faithful, 'Father, Dear Father' is on episode four hundred. Several other writers are working on the series these days, but every time they record an episode, the original creators get a fee.

Small story: when the movie of 'FDF' went to Johannesburg, it outgrossed 'Jaws', which was playing at the same time. They were queuing round the block to see what the radio characters looked like. Pointless, really, because their radio version uses completely different, local actors.

Oh, yes, we had a piece of the film grosses, too, as well as a film script fee.

Are you feeling encouraged? There's more, and this really is the cream on top of the jam.

Whilst the American networks won't buy the tapes of UK comedy shows (two nations divided by a common language), they have been known to buy the *idea*. Several times in recent years the American companies CBS, NBC and ABC have bought the format rights to successful UK sitcoms. They then remake the shows, often using the original scripts, adapted by American writers and using an American cast and American directors.

'Till Death Us Do Part', 'Steptoe and Son', 'Man About the House' and 'Keep It in the Family' have all had this treatment.

So have many other UK shows. They've not all worked out, but enough of them have become smash hits to make the networks keen to continue the practice.

And if you get a hit in America, you really do need the services of a good lawyer and a chartered accountant.

Australia, too, has bought the format rights to UK shows, and so has Western Germany. Even more money . . .

This chapter should do two things for you. It should take your breath away with the financial possibilities of a successful series, which must start with a good pilot programme.

And it should remind you that you're in competition for these pots of gold with every other professional comedy writer in the business. You've got to be as good as they are. All the things you've read so far have become second nature to the pro-writers. They might not call them 'weenies' or 'time factors' but they know what they are. And now you do, too. Let us continue.

I know I haven't finished the page, but I want a drink and I want it now!

11 : who are all these people?

At this stage it might be a good idea to introduce you to some of the people who will be responsible for turning your words into a show. You've sold the script to a television company and dozens of folk are going to be intimately involved in it before it gets onto the screen. Your work isn't over yet, but now that the script is on the production line, you're only one of a team.

First and foremost is your producer/director. The reason he often has two titles is because he's doing two jobs. Think of him as Jekyll and Hyde. The production half of his job involves him agreeing and controlling the budget, booking the performers, overseeing all the arrangements for the recording facilities, the dubbing, the editing. It's the managerial part. Sometime during all this he segues into being the director. That's the creative part. It's the half that rehearses the performers, argues with the writer, does the camera script and is in charge of the control box during the recording.

It's a complex job and in some companies you'll find it being done by two people. But mostly one person does the lot. To make life easier, let's call him the director from now on, and let's assume he's a male. There are very few female comedy directors.

Directors are the highly paid elite of television and most of the comedy directors do nothing but sitcoms and variety shows. They don't switch to drama or documentaries. They're also on residuals these days. If your show (or their show, as they'll think of it) gets repeated or sells abroad, they get a percentage of their original fee, too. Not of any format deals, though. It's still your show in that respect.

To be fair, most comedy directors really do know what they're doing. You, at the moment, do not. So leave it to him to block out the movements of the show during rehearsals, to decide whether your bit of visual business is funny, to make the whole thing work. That's his job, he's in charge.

Your director will have a PA, a producer's assistant, almost always a female. At first glance she'll appear to be a secretary, but that's only a minor part of her job. She's the one who will arrange auditions, draw up the cast list and provisional rehearsal schedules, type the camera script, time the rehearsals daily and generally keep her finger on the pulse of the whole show. At the actual recording she'll be timing everything down to the last second, even as she'll be calling out the hundreds of camera shots. She'll be there at the dubbing and editing, reminding the director of the cuts he wanted to make. She's his left-hand man, so to speak.

His right-hand man is his floor manager. This gentleman will also be around at all rehearsals. He'll even step in, should the director have to leave, and rehearse the cast himself. Most directors don't let this happen too often . . . their floor manager might be better at it than they are. The floor manager will certainly think so. He'd like to be a director himself. A lot of them make it, too, since they're in an ideal position to learn the ropes. A floor manager, almost always a male, is the person who 'cues' the performers. That is, he gives them the signal when to start talking at the beginning of a scene, when to make their entrance and so on. He'll also 'cue' sound effects, such as doorbells, or anything that isn't being fed in through the control box, anything that hasn't been recorded on tape, such as the sound of an offstage car smash.

But his big moment comes on the recording night. He's in charge of the studio floor. I should explain here that a television studio is divided into two parts: the studio floor itself, where all the sets and the lights and the cameras are, where all the action takes place in front of your studio audience; and the other half is the control room, where the director sits, flanked by his technical supervisors, his PA and his hyperventilating writer. On the night, all the director's instructions are given to the floor manager, via a 'deaf-aid' type walkie-talkie intercom.

Your floor manager frequently has to be something of a diplomat, especially during a retake. He'll turn your director's bellowed, 'Tell the silly cow to do it again,' into the more tactful, 'Absolutely perfect, darling. Couldn't be better, really. Could we try one more little takette?'

During the rehearsal and recording period the floor manager will work closely with the stage manager. (Sometimes called the assistant floor manager, to their chagrin.) Basically, the stage manager is in charge of rehearsals and the actual staging of the show. He/she will make sure that the layout on the floor of the rehearsal room (usually marked out in coloured tapes) will match the sets in the studio when they all get round to recording. Your rehearsals do not take place in the studio. It'd be too expensive and anyway other shows will be recording there. Your show will be rehearsed in any available drill hall, scout hall or gymnasium that happens to be close to the director's house.

The sets will be marked out on the floor and any bits and pieces of furniture that are lying around will be utilised. Sometimes the stage manager will arrange for some furniture to be brought in, along with any tricky props that will be needed on the night. Generally, rehearsals take place in tacky surroundings with tatty props substituting for the real thing. Many a grand banquet scene has been rehearsed on a three-legged card-table with two chipped mugs and paper plates.

The stage manager will also keep a careful note of any script changes that take place during rehearsal. He/she will prompt the cast, especially in the early stages when they're trying to 'get rid of the book', usually before they've learned it. Again, on the night, the stage manager really starts to buzz around, making sure that everything on the stage is where it should be. The actor, concentrating like crazy on his words, is quite liable to trip over a coffee-table if it's not in exactly the same place as it was during rehearsals.

The sets for your show will have been the responsibility of the designer. This man (or, less frequently, woman) will have read your script carefully some months before the recording date. He'll have drawn up a set of floor plans, fitting your five or six sets into the studio, sometimes adjusting their sizes so they'll all squeeze in. He and the director (and perhaps you) will have gone over these plans, checking that everything is as the script says. We're assuming here that the script is workable. You can't have a kitchen leading off a bedroom if it's supposed to be a normal house.

The designer will also have made small cardboard models of each set, and frequently he'll have done sketches, too. All you'll have written in your script is 'INT: LIVING ROOM: DAY:' and perhaps described it as having a chintz three-piece suite. He has to turn it into reality, choosing wallpaper, carpets, doors, tables, pictures and all the paraphernalia that a normal living-room will contain. He also has to arrange for the building and assembling of the sets.

Major television companies have carpentry shops on-site. They'll do most of the work in their workshops, only transferring the sets to the studio on the day before the recording. Sets are one of the biggest items of cost in any television production. Another reason for keeping them down to a minimum.

The designer will work closely with the prop buyer, who will arrange for the chintz three-piece suite to be available. He'll dress the basic set, providing the books, lampshades, etc. A better name for him might be prop renter, since he'll normally rent most of the stuff from outside firms specialising in such things. Both the designer and the prop buyer will often be on the staff of the production company. Their wages will have to be allowed for in the budget of your show.

These five people will be the ones you'll see most of during the course of rehearsing and recording your first and any subsequent show. The only one that you personally need to pay any attention to is the director, though the others can often be helpful and they're better as friends than enemies.

If you've included any filmed inserts in the show, you'll also meet the location manager. His job is to scout around and find the little Gothic church with the seventeenth-century triforium that you specified. He'd like to find it within a mile or two of the studios, otherwise the cost of trucking everybody out to Cornwall will be astronomical. You may have to settle for an eighteenth-century clerestory and hope it still gets laughs.

You'll also meet literally dozens of other people. Amongst them are the wardrobe mistress, responsible for all the clothes; the make-up artists; the sound and lighting and camera crews; the boom operators (A boom is a microphone on a long pole. You've all seen them on your screens. You shouldn't have.); the vision mixer (who mixes down the four camera pictures to the one that's being recorded); the dressers (who help the performers change clothes quickly); the scene shifters; the props men; the camera and lighting grips (so called because if they catch you moving something they should be moving, they grip you in a painful place); the studio electrician; the security commissionaires, etc. etc. Dozens of people.

See what you've started?!

12: The performers, bless 'em

The first performer your studio audience will meet isn't even in the show.

He's the warm-up man. Often a stand-up comic himself, his job is to turn this miscellaneous bunch of singles, couples, family foursomes and coach parties into a genuine, *bona fide*, ready to cackle studio audience. He's got a quarter of an hour to do so.

Fifteen minutes before the studio recording begins, he'll attempt to take three hundred and fifty strangers and turn them into friends. He'll do it with a mixture of patter, gags and information. The warm-up man is the unsung hero of sitcom and sketch shows.

I recall one, though, who totally blew all his own hard work by announcing with sincere emotion, 'Ladies and gentlemen, I've just heard some tragic news. President Kennedy has been assassinated! And now, on with the show . . .'

Your warm-up man will also familiarise the audience with the studio facilities, helping them relax.

Hanging over your head you'll see several large television monitors, held up there by chewing gum and string. We've never had one fall down . . . yet. Also up there you'll see half a dozen microphones. These are there to pick up your shrieks of laughter and your spontaneous applause, which will be signalled by the floor manager. Now, these are very sensitive but – they've never yet made one that can pick up a *smile*. So, if you understand a joke, laugh! If you *think* you understand a joke, laugh! If you *don't* understand a joke, laugh anyway and work it out on the way home. We've got two minutes to go, if anybody wants to . . .

You get the idea. Your warmer-upper will keep the audience 'on the boil' during the inevitable tape-stops and retakes. Tape-stops are planned, retakes aren't. They happen fairly often on every show, usually because of a technical problem or because a performer fluffs a line by getting his tangue all tongled up. Funnily enough, an audience will often laugh more at a retake than at the original. Sometimes you'll get a retake of a retake of a retake. After about six it gets embarrassing and you may have to settle for less than perfection.

A bit of visual business in one of our shows involved Ian Carmichael aiming a revolver at Patrick Cargill. It was actually a cigarette lighter and when he pulled the trigger a little flame was supposed to come from the barrel of the gun. It didn't work. After ten retakes, it finally did what it was supposed to do. The audience burst into delighted applause, ruining the take and we had to do it again.

And now, finally, we're talking about the performers, the actors and actresses that will make or break your script. You may feel strongly that, without specific performers playing your lead characters, the show won't work. As I've said before, it's a good thing to write with somebody in mind if only to keep the part consistent. But it's quite possible that you won't be able to get the people that you want.

You will certainly have the opportunity to discuss the casting with your director. He may disagree with your opinions and offer alternatives. He may disagree for all sorts of reasons. He may know that the performer you want is an alcoholic and can't learn lines, he may be in some other sitcom that you don't know about, he may hate the sight of the particular actress you want, he may be dead.

We have to be practical here. All your ideas about casting will have come from seeing performers on your own television screen, or in films or theatre. You won't know that so-and-so has just had a hit film in America and won't touch another sitcom in Britain. Or so-and-so is fed up playing comedy and is touring with 'Waiting for Godot' in New Zealand. He or she may simply be unavailable for the rehearsal and recording period.

I'm speaking here of the major roles, not the bit parts. The alternative performers that your director suggests may horrify you. Tell him so, it's all you can do. Between you you'll reach some sort of happy compromise.

In most cases, I'd again advise you to go along with what your director feels is right. You have to trust his judgement. He knows more than you do, he's got a better idea of the 'chemistry' between some performers and the 'marquee value' of others. The final decision is his, anyway.

On the smaller parts, the waiter, the taxi driver and so on, your director will have a small group of reliable performers that he's worked with before, his own little repertory company. He'll either use these or he'll audition.

If he auditions, try to get involved. It's fascinating to see how different performers interpret the same words. Every reading will be different and for the first time you'll hear your words spoken by someone other than yourself. It may depress you or it may elate you. Either way, it's all expreience.

On the other hand, you may get the people you want. Our director may agree wholeheartedly that Les Dawson would be fabulous as Wilf, Dandy Nicholls would be perfect as Hilda. And Les and Dandy agree to do it. It can happen.

One thing is for sure. Somehow or other your show will be cast. Performers will be signed up and you'll enter the next phase, the rehearsals.

⑬ Rehearsals

Usually there are five days of rehearsals, followed by one day in the studio, in the evening of which you will record the show. This can vary slightly. You might get two days in the studio if you've got a lot of scenes that need to be pre-recorded without an audience. For instance, if there are under-age children written into the script and they feature strongly. If you pre-recorded their scenes in the afternoon of your recording day you'd have no time to have a proper run-through of all the other scenes. You'd need two days.

What follows is a day-by-day breakdown of events in the rehearsal week of a typical pilot situation comedy. The designer has done his floor plan, you've done any rewrites that were required and the cast has been finalised. Everybody will have been given a production schedule and they'll know that your rehearsal venue is the Fox and Firkin, an old pub just round the corner from your director's home. It has a good-sized reception room at the back, with a floor big enough to take a wedding party, a dance or a number of set layouts. The Fox and Firkin manager will be picking up a couple of hundred pounds for the use of his hall. He's happy. He might even allow you to use his car park. That could be useful, since your performers will be coming from all over the place.

Day one: Rehearsals have been called for 10 a.m. The stage manager will have arrived early. She'll have taped the floor with the set layouts, placed any bits of furniture in position and put the kettle on. She'll have pushed several tables together, with enough chairs round for everyone to sit on. This is for the table read-through.

The PA will turn up at about quarter to ten, carrying enough scripts for everyone, in case they forget to bring the ones that were posted to them. You'll arrive at about the same time, as will the floor manager.

The various performers will start to drift in during the next ten minutes, greeting each other with great sincerity if they've worked together before. (Sincerity is the most important part of acting ... once they've learned to fake that, they're fine.) The wardrobe and make-up people will arrive, so will the designer. The director will arrive at quarter past. His excuse will be that, because he lives so close, he doesn't have time to hurry up when he's late. Everybody will chuckle appreciatively.

At one rehearsal, my director was suffering from a dreadful hangover and knew he was going to be very late. He phoned up and asked me to apologise and tell the cast he was having trouble with his car. I did so. When he finally turned up, our leading lady asked him what exactly was wrong with the car. He squinted at her blearily. 'I couldn't *see* it,' he said.

Then they'll have their read-through. Everybody will sit round the long table and the actors will briskly read through the whole script. Some actors like to give a performance on a 'read', others don't. Either way, you're hearing the whole thing done by professionals for the first time. Despite all your care, you'll almost certainly realise that you've made a few mistakes. The spoken word *is* different from the written one.

At this point you'll all have a discussion, and you'll get the chance to correct the small mistakes. The actors, too, may have a few points they'd like to make. It's a bit disconcerting to find them discussing your script through the director, but that's usually the way it's done. If you've got something to say to the actors, you do the same. Don't give an actor notes. Give them to the director and if he agrees with you, he'll pass them on. It's democratic, if frustrating.

If you don't agree with the actors' notes, say so. It's your script. You've worked on the thing for weeks, you know it better than any of them. At the same time, an experienced actor can bring up something that you hadn't considered, so do listen.

At this discussion, the make-up and wardrobe girls will talk about their plans. Pay attention. Do you really want your leading man in a velvet smoking-jacket and a monocle, or did you see him in a woolly dressing-gown and granny glasses?

The PA will have timed this first read. It should run at about twenty minutes for an ITV sitcom, or twenty-four for a BBC show. It's going to 'spread' as it's rehearsed and two minutes or so will be allowed for studio audience reaction.

The set designer will check that everything is as it should be, then he'll split, along with the wardrobe and make-up people.

The director and the performers will now get down to blocking out the moves. They'll start rehearsing properly, going over each scene again and again before moving on to the next. It's quite possible that they won't block out the whole show today. It's a slow business. You don't need to stay but you'll probably want to. If you do stay, be unobtrusive. For you, this is a learning process, an opportunity to find out more about how a comedy show is put together. Invaluable experience.

A break for lunch, probably in the saloon bar of the Fox and Firkin, then back to rehearsals again. Some directors prefer to work only until about two o'clock, and then break for the day. The performers will go home and start to study and learn their parts.

Day two: The production schedule for the day will have one word on it: 'Rehearse'. That's exactly what they will do. They'll block out what they didn't block out yesterday. Then they'll start at the beginning and carefully go through the whole show all over again. They wouldn't expect you to turn up. If you intend to be there, tell your director the previous day. Small changes will begin to happen at this stage. Perhaps an actor will realise that he hasn't got enough dialogue to cover a move. He has two choices. Either he moves faster or he starts to ad-lib, to make up words that aren't in your script. If they all start adding lines – and it can get to be contagious – you'll finish up with a show that's too long. It's up to the director to sort it out, to start the move earlier, or phone you and ask for an extra line. He'll probably take the easy way out and let the actor ad-lib.

The PA will continue to time each scene, comparing the timings with the read-through. The director is beginning to think about his camera script, to orchestrate the movements of his cameras, to figure out which one takes each shot. In the afternoon, the wardrobe lady may take the leading actress out shopping with her. They have to buy a dress for one particular scene. Another chunk of the budget gone.

Day three: More of the same. Some of the performers will be word perfect by now. They'll have discarded their scripts. Any prompts that are needed will be supplied by the stage manager.

It's likely that one of the actors will have to leave early. He's got to go and do a voice over for a radio commercial. His agent will have mentioned this when he took the part in the first place. The floor manager will step in and play his role while he's absent. He knows the moves; he's been watching the director like a hawk.

There may be a problem with one of the elderly bit part supporting actresses. She can't get a line right. As a matter of fact, she's not playing the part at all well. Should she be replaced before it's too late? Let's see how she is tomorrow.

Two of the performers have worked out an hilarious bit of visual business for one of their scenes. They play it for the director. He hates it. They agree that it wasn't all that good and forget it. You don't know any of this. You're not there.

The director is scribbling notes on his own copy of the script. He's almost finished working out what he wants his cameras to do.

The PA, still timing everything, says that the last rehearsal was twenty-eight minutes long. Perfect. No, wait a minute! She hasn't allowed for the opening credits sequence. It's two minutes over. Let's speed everything up or get the writer to cut something.

One more complete rehearsal. It's still too long. There is one possible cut, but let's leave it until tomorrow.

Day four: The usual 10 a.m. rehearsal call. The elderly supporting actress has brought her pet poodle with her. It gets lonely when she's working. It growls at the floor manager.

One complete rehearsal, then the first outsider will see the show. The cast will do a complete run-through for him. He's there so he can anticipate any problems of lighting on the recording night. He's the lighting supervisor.

This is the best time for you to turn up again. The actors have all laid aside their scripts and there's still time for you to cut or add or disagree with what's been added.

The lighting run goes well, apart from the elderly actress who's still having trouble with her lines. And the show has spread even more. It's now three minutes too long. The director isn't too worried. He can see a good cut that he can do later, after the show has been recorded. He can edit it electronically. On the other hand, he may ask you for your suggestions.

When it comes to cutting your script at this stage, take a hard look at the beginning and the end of each individual scene. If you do a major cut in the middle of a scene, it can often foul up the whole flow of the scene as it's been rehearsed. Better to lop a bit off the beginning or end, or, if possible, cut a whole scene out.

The pet poodle bites the director as he's giving a note to the elderly actress. He can't replace her now or it'll look vindictive.

The set designer phones up. There's a threat of an industrial dispute in the carpentry shop. You may have to do the whole show without doorknobs. Apart from that, the sets are almost completed.

The director goes home to work on his camera script. It has to be ready by the following morning. The PA may be working overtime tonight. She's the one who has to type it.

Day five: Yet another run-through. Everybody in the cast is word perfect, with one exception.

The elderly actress is upset. The manager of the Fox and Firkin has stopped her on the way in. 'Didn't you used to be Celia Wetherby?' he said. She graciously pointed out that she still is. 'I thought so,' he said, 'but I didn't want to offend you.'

The second run of the day will be in front of about a dozen cynics. These are the cameramen and sound technicians. They generally pride themselves on not laughing at anything except the rude bits. Actually, they're not there to laugh. This technical run, as it's called, is to familiarise them all with what they're going to be doing on the night. They've each got a copy of the camera script, with all their instructions typed out on the left-hand side of the page. The PA is yawning.

The designer turns up. The dispute is still simmering but the sets are being erected on the studio floor. It's possible that you won't have any doors, though. The management are in negotiation with the union concerned. There's nothing anyone can do except perhaps run through the scene that features your elderly actress. This time she almost gets the words right.

14 : On the day

This is it, studio day. 0900 hours. Your sets will have been erected, maybe even complete with doors and doorknobs if the dispute has been resolved. The furniture and all the other 'dressing' is being placed into position. The stage manager is buzzing about like a bee on elastic.

The audience seating has been trucked in and is being bolted together. Yesterday they were recording a drama in this very studio and they didn't need the seats since they didn't have an audience. In fact, some of the drama sets are still stacked against the wall, ready to be taken back to the carpentry shop and dismantled.

It's going to be a long day today, almost twelve hours of solid work on everybody's part.

1015. The actors will begin to arrive. They'll sit in their various small dressing-rooms, waiting for their call. The first studio run-through in the proper sets will begin at ten-thirty. The actors won't wear make-up or costume for this run. It's not necessary. This run is mainly for the camera and sound crews. It's known as the 'stagger' because they'll stop and start a lot as they familiarise themselves with the shots they have to take. It's their rehearsal.

1030. Up in the control room, overlooking the studio floor, the director and his PA will be seated in front of a battery of television monitors, each showing a different picture from each of the four operating cameras. There will also be a stand-by camera in case of a breakdown. The transmission screen is showing the picture that will be recorded. The vision mixer, on the right of the director, controls which picture gets on to the transmission screen.

As this run proceeds, the director will be constantly nipping down the stairs to the studio floor to sort out any problems as they arise. Camera 2 can't get across for his shot 90. Maybe camera 4 can make it. The boom operator can't get close enough, without being in shot, to pick up the sound when they come through the front door. We'll use a pin-mike hidden behind the door-frame.

This first studio run usually looks totally chaotic. It's hard to imagine that in less than ten hours it will be in any fit state to be played in front of an audience.

1300. You're about halfway through the 'stagger' but it's lunchtime and everything has to stop for an hour.

1400. Back to work, back to the camera rehearsal. The actors are getting used to the sets by now. They know where their 'marks' are, where they pause and turn, where the various cameras are going to be. They know when the camera that's pointing at them is actually working: a little red light glows on top of it.

Various other people from the studios will drop by, sit in the audience, watch a little of the rehearsals, perhaps laugh at some of the dialogue. Very encouraging. The floor manager will constantly be calling for quiet. 'People are *working*!'

The lighting supervisor will be adjusting his lights to give the best possible results on screen. The sound supervisor will be worrying about the pin-mike on the door-frame. It's not as reliable, the sound isn't quite as good as a boom-mike will give. It'll have to do, though.

1600. Everything has to stop. With luck you'll have finished the 'stagger'. Even if you haven't you've got to stop for a tea break and to get ready for your penultimate performance, the 'dress run'.

The technical boys 'line-up' the cameras. That is, they make sure they all match, that the colours on one are exactly the same as the colours on the rest, that the technical quality on all four is identical.

The actors snatch a cup of tea and move into make-up and wardrobe.

1700. The dress rehearsal. This is a full-scale run, in make-up and costumes, done exactly as the show will be done later on in the evening. The only difference is that there will be no audience. This is the run that you should come to today. It's too late to do anything but the most minor changes, but you should see it, on the screen, before the recording.

The warm-up man has arrived. He'll sit through this run, making notes on his copy of the script. 'Tape run or possible stop here.' 'Intro Celia Wetherby BEFORE her scene.'

You've got an hour, maybe an hour and a quarter, to do this dress run. It's the same amount of time that you'll have to record the show later. This includes all the costume changes. To change from pyjamas to a business suit can easily take ten minutes. Remember that when you're writing your script, and keep your costume changes to a minimum.

You'll probably sit in the control box during this run. Keep quiet, even when the elderly lady actress fluffs every single one of her lines.

Apart from Celia, everything goes relatively smoothly. No real problems. The chaos of the 'stagger' has somehow transformed itself into a well-drilled routine. Only one thing wrong. It doesn't seem at all funny.

1815. The director will give his final notes to the cast, usually fairly small points. 'When you stand up in scene 3, give it a beat before you move off.' 'Take a cue from the floor manager on that soda syphon squirt.'

Then it's supper-time, for those who feel like eating. The technical boys will be up in the canteen, stuffing themselves on subsidised sausages and chips. No nerves there, all seasoned professionals. The actors will usually settle for a cup of tea. Tension is beginning to build up. I once asked a well-known performer how he got over his pre-show nerves. 'Well,' he said, 'I always imagine that the first three rows all owe me money!'

1915. The cast report back for make-up and costume. Those who are so inclined will take a surreptitious nip of something alcoholic. A 'phlegm cutter', they call it.

The camera line-up is checked yet again. The audience is beginning to queue up outside the studios. One or two coaches
have arrived.

1930. The security commissionaires usher the audience into
their seats. They take pot-luck in where they sit, the tickets are
numbered but the seats aren't. Family and friends of the people
connected with the show will have a 'reserved' section somewhere
near the front and centre.

The audience goggle at the unfamiliar setting. At least half of
them will never have been in a studio before. The sets are not
yet lit. Studio lights are hot, no point in building up the temper-
ature of the studio unnecessarily. The audience buzz, a little
overawed by the whole thing. Some of them have written in for
tickets to any show. This is the one they've got. Others belong to
clubs and organisations. They've been contacted by the ticket
unit and offered block bookings. They've accepted. It's good to
have several coach parties in. People laugh more when they're in
a group.

The ticket unit staff are helping to seat the audience. They
have a list of all the coach parties. They'll give it to the warm-up
man and he'll use it in his opening chat.

1945. The warm up man strolls out, plucks the hand mike
from the stand, starts to work. Friendly, unassuming but insist-
ent.

> Good evening, ladies and gentlemen. Dear God . . . let's
> try it again. GOOD EVENING, LADIES AND
> GENTLEMEN! That's better. Welcome to Studio 1.
> Let's get to know each other. All turn round and shake
> the hand of the person in the seat behind you . . .

They turn round, only to find that the person behind them is, of
course, doing the same. Laughter. The ice is being broken.

Behind the sets, the performers are grouped together, listening.
Is it going to be a good audience? Up on the gantry outside the
control box you and the director will be looking down, studying

the audience yourselves. Seems about right. Not too many old people, not too many young. A good cross-section. The laughter seems a bit 'feathery', though. No 'shriekers' in tonight. A 'shrieker' is someone, usually a woman, with a high-pitched laugh. One of these can sometimes spoil the whole sound balance. You'd have to adjust the pick-up on the audience microphone above her head if she was really shrill.

The main members of the cast are introduced. They come out front, take a quick bow, perhaps say a few words. Everybody is anxious to get started. The set lights come on. Very bright.

2000. The actors take up their positions for their opening scene, just as rehearsed. The warm-up man fades into the shadows.

Up in the control box fingers are crossed, on buttons, on switches, on the stopwatch. The round clock on the transmission screen is ticking away the seconds. This clock doesn't exist except on that screen. It's an electronic image. At twenty seconds to VTR (video tape recording) time, the floor manager's voice is heard, reading the title: 'Hilda and Wilf. Take 1, scene 1.' At ten seconds there's a final sound check, an electronic 'blip' from the clock. 'Stand by telecine. Stand by grams . . .' We're off.

The first thing the audience will see on their monitor screens is the identifying logo and music of the production company doing the show. This will be followed by the titles, credits and theme music of your show, if they've been done in advance. If not, a simple caption card will identify the show and the vision mixer will go straight into the opening shot of scene 1. The floor manager cues the actors and . . . you're in business.

Not much reaction from the audience on the first few lines. They're still settling down. They can't see all that much of the action on the floor, unless the set is directly in front of them. Even then, there are bulky cameras and the sound boom trolley between them and the performers. So they'll be watching the nearest monitor most of the time.

Here comes your 'cowcatcher'. It gets a big laugh, thank heavens. This could be fun. Oh-oh. Here's the elderly lady actress with her first longish speech. She's word-perfect. Absolutely marvellous. This completely throws her fellow performer and he dries up, stumbles on a phrase, says, 'Oh, sh*t! Whoops . . . sorry!'

The director jumps in quickly. 'Keep the tape running! Let's pick up on . . . er . . . shot 23, Celia's close up on 2. In five. One, two, three . . .'

The audience loves retakes. They're in on a secret that the viewers at home will never see. It's even been known for an actor deliberately to fluff a line to get the audience going, to get their sympathy.

The pick-up on the retake is fine. The scene continues, with the performers doing their incredible balancing act, that fine line between playing to the audience and pretending they're not there. End of scene 1. Two minutes in the can. Tape stop for a costume change. The warm-up man steps forward again. 'That's all. Thank you for coming. Goodnight!' Laughter.

And so it goes on, until the last shot has been taken and the closing credits roll up on the monitor screens. A short wait as the technicians spot-check the recording tape (they've been doing it all through the show) to make sure there have been no technical hitches. 'We're just popping the film down to the chemist to get it developed,' says the warm-up man. It's a 'clear'. It's all over.

The PA tots up her final scene timings. The show is one minute, thirty-two seconds over. Easily fixed on the editing session next week. Everybody to the studio bar for the post-mortem. When can we start the series?

15/ A short pause for another breather

All you would-be sketch writers can now move to the front of the hall. Thank you for being so patient, I hope it wasn't too boring for you. Sitcom writers can fall out and slope off for a while. I'd like you back in time for the last chapter. Or you can hang about. You might learn something.

A lot of writers do write both sketches and situation comedy. Some of them feel that a sitcom is just a string of connected sketches, anyway. They may have a point. After all, 'Till Death . . .' or 'Last of the Summer Wine' weren't exactly stiff with plot. A lot of the time they were a series of vignettes.

And a good sketch should give you the feeling that the characters in it existed *before* and will continue to exist afterwards, that you've dipped into their life for three or four minutes, rather than half an hour.

The difference in the writing approach are what we're going to look at in the next few chapters.

16 - I'd rather write sketches

Great! Why not? Almost everything you've just read applies equally to comedy sketch writing. Most new writers (and some established ones) are a little daunted at the prospect of filling a whole half hour with plot and character *and* gags. It's got to be easier to write a three- or four-minute piece, with a good strong tag. Or even several quickies, those ten- or fifteen-second visual gags that feature in many sketch shows.

The snag is, if it is easier, then there's sure to be more writers doing it and the competition to sell your stuff is going to be just as fierce. Let's take a look at the market-place.

Obviously, there are many different types of sketch series but we can initially divide them into two broad categories: the Old and the New. I'm not talking about the quality of the writing or the gags. I mean that the traditional kind of sketch/variety shows, usually centred around a particular performer, are still going strong. And the newer series, which feature a group of performers, and are frequently more satirical or topical in their content, are also very popular.

In between these two extremes are a whole range of shows that use short pieces of material and which may be open to outside contributions. Some of the series are half an hour long and some are an hour. Some use musical material, some don't. I wish I could tell you that they're all looking for material from you, but they're not.

Let me tell you how a lot of sketch shows get started. Unlike situation comedies, a writer doesn't send in a complete half-hour script, or get commissioned to write a whole series on his own.

Sketch shows are more of a team effort, with many writers contributing bits and pieces. It's not true in all cases, but in most cases, this is how a sketch series gets off the ground.

A head of light entertainment takes a look at his schedule for next year. He sees that there are gaps. He also sees that the balance of what he's doing is tipped towards sitcoms or quiz shows. He calls in his staff producers/directors and they discuss the possibility of getting a little more variety (with a small 'v') into the schedules. How about a series of sketch shows? Fine. Who's coming up that's new? Who's been around for a while and hasn't yet had a series? Anything on radio that seems promising? Who's in it? Perhaps one director has been itching to do a series with Frankie Howerd. Is he available, is he interested? What about John Cleese? (This last question *always* comes up.)

Let's assume that the H. of L.E. agrees with one of his directors who wants to do a series with an up-and-coming stand-up comedian called Harvey Wallbanger.

Harvey has been in the business for some time. He's an ex-school-teacher who used to work the northern clubs at night. He's been spotted by a radio producer and has done a short, successful radio series called 'Wallbanger's World'. He's also been featured in several local TV shows, doing a three-minute stand-up spot. He's done two summer seasons, playing second comic on the bill, and he's won a TV talent show called 'Newcomers'. He's ripe and he's ready and eager to do his own TV series. Why wouldn't he be? It'll quadruple his money in the clubs.

The director sits down with a blank sheet of paper and writes at the top 'The Harvey Wallbanger Show. Six half hours'.

He's a creative director. He wants to make this sketch show different from all the others. Special, faster, funnier. I mean, very few directors sit down to do a samey, ordinary, slower, unfunny show. Though, looking at some of the ones that are around, I could be wrong . . .

Anyway, his first big problem is to find writers. He doesn't know about you yet. So, he gets out his list of favourite scribblers, people he's worked with before, people he knows he can rely on. Eddie and Spike and Barry and Eric. He phones them up, checks whether they'd like to contribute to 'The Harvey Wallbanger Show'.

If they're not already swamped with work and they'd like to contribute, he'll book all these writers for a fixed amount of material. Say, five minutes each for all six shows. If they fancy doing a little more, he'll buy that, too. He knows that he'll almost certainly get more from this group, they're not going to write with a stopwatch in their hands. But he's guaranteed to pay each of them for, and they've agreed to provide, half an hour's material for the series.

The blessed Writers' Guild will not allow any one of them to be paid less than £2,283 for this half hour of sketches, quickies, stand-up material or whatever. They will certainly be paid a lot more – they're well-established writers. And in one swoop the director has got the equivalent of two-thirds of his series written.

He may not be that lucky. Eddie, Spike and Eric may be too busy to supply anything at all. And Barry wants to think about it. So, the director will move down his list, trying a few other people. He may even phone a literary agent or two, tell them about the new show, ask if they've got any writers on their books who'd like to contribute. He'll perhaps get the studio publicity department to arrange for a news item in the 'Television Today' section of *The Stage* weekly newspaper, mentioning that he's looking for material. If he does, he'll be swamped with unsuitable scripts from all sorts of people who think they can write. Some of the sketches will be rather dog-eared and 'Tommy' or 'Ronnie' will have been crossed out and 'Harvey' written in.

Harvey himself may know a few comedy writers. They've been supplying him with material for his club act (usually too blue for television, though). Still, the director might decide to book them for a couple of minutes per show. He has a big enough writing budget to pay for material that he may not use. And all sketch shows have a certain amount of 'wastage' or 'stand-by' material: 'We'll use *that* bit if we can't get anything better.'

Eventually he'll have gathered together his regular team of writers. Half a dozen is normal. He may even get Barry, if he allows him to be script editor and pays him accordingly.

It's worth pausing for a moment to consider the role of the script editor. He's often a well-established writer who is interested in the production side of the business. Of course he can write, but he can do more than that. He can work closely with the director and formulate a show. He can give it a style and identity of its own. He also knows a lot of other writers (including a few newer ones the director has never heard of) and can phone them up on a first-name basis. 'What've you got in your files? Any quickies that Dave Allen wouldn't do? Can I take a look?'

Sometimes the script editor will have a different title. He'll be an associate producer or a production associate. No matter; what a good one does is to take the script problems off a director's back and allow him to concentrate on all the other aspects of the series.

So there we are. One director, one star, six writers and a script editor. They'll have many meetings, with and without Harvey, discussing the series, kicking around ideas, trying to give the series its own style of comedy. And gradually the usable material file will begin to thicken as they each go away and write their own pieces. It's still two months before the first recording.

Very interesting, you're thinking. But what's it got to do with me?

Everything, because this is the walled market-place that you, or any other new writer, has to break into. By setting it out I can make you see how it's going to be, how difficult it is to become part of the established order. Quite simply, your material has to force its way in. Nobody will come looking for it.

The frustrating thing for new writers is that they only get to know about a new series when it goes on the air. By then it's almost always too late, all the material has been contracted for and written. Sure, there may be a second series but that could be six months or a year away. And the old regulars will be writing that, too.

We'll talk about the best way of breaking into the market-place later. Right now let's consider exactly what it is that you want to write.

⑰ Juggling Soot

The previous chapter may have disheartened you a bit. It wasn't intended to. Barry, Eric, Spike and Eddie were all on the outside, looking in, at one time. So was I. None of us had a brother-in-law who bought comedy scripts. That was then, you may say. But now the market-place is much, much bigger. Once you get your foot in the door, if you're any good at all, you'll be dragged inside so fast you'll leave scorch marks on the concrete. I'll say it again, the television companies really *do* need many new writers. OK? OK.

As we did with situation comedy, it's a good idea to analyse a little before we get down to writing any material for sketch shows. It's rather like juggling soot, but we ought to look at the whole content of non-sitcom shows and see the components. One of them may attract you more than the others. For instance, you may turn out to be brilliant at one of the hardest things to write, stand-up comedy.

Stand-up comedy

Or, in Dave Allen's case, sit-down comedy. It goes back to the music-halls and even further. I'm sure the philosophers in ancient Greece used to spice their homilies with a sly crack or two about Diogenes and his mother-in-law. Most sketch/variety shows that feature a stand-up comic will usually have a five-minute stand-up spot at the front end of the show. One of the reasons it's tricky to write is because the comedian doing it often has such a strong style and you have to go along with it. Any patter that you wrote for, say, Frankie Howerd, would sound wrong if somebody else did it.

FRANK (TAKES OPENING APPLAUSE). Thank you, thank you. May I say, first of all, that it's a great pleasure and a privilege for you to be here with me tonight. I'd like to try something now that hasn't been done for years. This is a crossbow ... and this is an apple. Now, I shall need one volunteer from the audience. To put the apple on his head. Just one volunteer, that's all. (THE AUDI-ENCE HAS BEEN TOLD NOT TO VOLUNTEER.) Just one. Think about it, while I put this razor sharp bolt into the crossbow. (DOES SO.) Anybody? No? Well, how about if the whole front row put apples on their heads? It would give me a better chance, wouldn't it? Not keen? All right ... one volunteer. Come on, now. This may be my last chance to try this ... my eyesight's going. One volunteer. (SEES SOMEONE IN AUDIENCE.) Ah, gentleman over there! Round of applause for the gentle-man! (APPLAUSE AS A MAN JOINS HIM FROM THE AUDIENCE. THE MAN HAS A CROSSBOW BOLT THROUGH HIS HEAD.) Oh, no. Not you! You were useless at rehearsals!

You can hear Frank saying it, right? Wrong. I cheated. We wrote that piece for Tommy Cooper. And he did it very well.

The purpose of this little deception was to show you that if a gag is funny, it can be done by several different people. Don't be overawed by anybody's style or reputation. A good gag can easily be adapted slightly, usually by the comedian himself, to suit anybody.

It's best to divide your stand-up patter, rather than run it all together, which suggests you want to sell the whole piece or nothing. Think of it from the director's or the script editor's point of view. It's easier to read if you lay it out something like this:

TOMMY. The wife's been on at me for months to grow a moustache ... but I won't let her.

TOMMY. I failed a breath test last week. I got disqualified from breathing for six months.

TOMMY. I looked in the mirror last night and . . . for the first time, I noticed a gleam of silver . . . just there. (SMOOTHS BACK HIS HAIR AT THE SIDE.) I'd left my cigarette case behind my ear!

TOMMY. I'd like to show you this. (HOLDS UP BLUE BANANA.) It's a blue banana. It's for people with yellow jaundice. It stops them eating their fingers.

Of course, there may be times when the patter is so low-key, so geared to the individual performer, that you have to run it all together. Here's a piece that really was written for Frankie Howerd. He's been introduced by David Frost, the host of the programme. You'll have to imagine David's fulsome introduction from Frank's reaction to it.

FRANK. Thank you, David. How kind, very nice, yes. Has he gone? (TO AUDIENCE.) Did you hear that 'good friend' bit? Lies. I've never met him before last week. I've seen him on the telly, of course. Who can avoid it? He's all right, I suppose. If you like the pushy type. He called me into his office . . . I say 'office' . . . a hundred yards long, fifty foot wide. And that's only the desk! Yes! He's got this paperweight. The Statue of Liberty, in solid silver. Life size! Anyway, I waded through the carpet and fell on my knees . . . it's a little custom he encourages. 'There's a lot of prestige in this show,' he said. I thought, 'Hullo, there's no money in it!' So, I said, 'I'm not going to be rushed into anything,' I said. I know my worth. Unfortunately, so did he, so here I am . . .

Notice the absence of 'Ooohs' and 'Aaahs'? Frank didn't want them written in for him. 'I can do that myself,' he used to say. 'Just give me the gags!'

Which is what stand-up routines are all about. Strong, new gags. Don't pinch them out of joke books or, if you do, twist them round so they're unrecognisable. D'you think Les Dawson or Jim Davidson won't have heard every old gag around? Of course they have. They don't need you to write them down and try to sell them.

A final word about stand-up stuff. It's no good just sending in half a dozen gags, even if they're all mint fresh. You'll need a couple of dozen to make it worth the postage. And it's a good thing to test the waters by sending in your stand-up stuff along with several sketches. That particular show might not need any stand-up material. You won't know until you've tried. Hedge your bet with some sketches and quickies.

Crosstalk

The patter between a double act – such as Morecombe and Wise – is a close relative of stand-up comedy. But I think you'll find it harder to sell, even if it seems easy to write. Superficially, M. & W. may have elements in common with, say, Cannon and Ball or Little and Large, but their relationships are basically very different.

If you'd ever listened to Eric and Ernie discussing their approach to crosstalk you'd realise how complex it is. Ernie has developed from being the comic half of the act (which he was when they first started), through being a feed, to being whatever it is he is today. He's now a completely rounded character in his own right, sometimes dumb, sometimes cunning, sometimes too clever for his own good. Eric has moved from being the gormless half to sometimes being the wiser one who protects his friend's ego, or punctures his pomposity. Occasionally he'll revert back to being a little gormless, when it suits him. A complex, ever-changing relationship, even inside a five-minute patter routine.

Very tricky to write, expecially for an outside contributor. Still, if you can't resist writing crosstalk, study the act you want to write for very, very carefully. Then send them several routines, not just one. There aren't all that many double acts on television, so it's a limited market. You could always watch out for a new double act, then concentrate on them. They won't have fully developed their relationship and could be glad of outside help.

GoOb eV*nong%$\frac{1}{02}$. A sudDden+ strIke bY t£E BBC TYp;isTs un&ioN haZ ca*uSed ChAos iN%'' th$\frac{1}{3}$ NeWQsroom@+ . . .

Linking material

Almost impossible for an outsider to write and sell. This is the chat that the host or the star of the show will use to introduce his guest singer or group. I know it's only a tiny part of the show but it still has to be written. A lot of shows still take the easy way out and do it absolutely straight. 'And now, a marvellous singer of marvellous songs . . .' doesn't make any great demands on anybody.

The guests often VTR their song(s) a day or two before the actual recording and the audience will watch it played back on the monitors. The host, however, will do the introduction live on the night. 'Ladies and gentlemen, the wonderful Fanny Tonsils . . .' he'll cry, waving towards a totally empty part of the stage and leading the applause. If I were you I'd forget about the linking material, at least until you get your foot through the door.

Novelty items

Under this heading I'd include anything that wasn't a sketch or a quickie. 'The Two Ronnies' and 'Not the Nine O'Clock News' use a lot of pseudo news items.

> RONNIE B. A lorryload of strawberries collided with a tankerful of cream on the A213, near Darlington. A police spokesman on the spot said, 'Scrumptious!'

Novelty items like the newsreader sketch help to break up the standard pattern of a sketch show. They introduce another element into the stand-up, sketch, quickie, quickie, sketch format. Most directors or script editors are on the lookout for something different. If you can think of a novely item then write up three or four of them, not just one. Show that your idea has got legs, that it can run.

The newsreader routine will be around for a long time because it's a good way of doing a string of quickfire gags. If you feel you can write them, then do avoid the temptation to be too topical. By the time you get your material accepted, it'll be dated. And most sketch shows are recorded weeks before they're transmitted.

A few further thoughts on novelty items. Song parodies may attract you. Putting new words to an old song can be funny, but make sure the song is out of copyright. It's not always possible to do because the people who wrote the original, or hold the copyright on it, won't give permission. Generally speaking, if the composer and lyricist of the song have been dead for fifty years, you're OK. It's out of copyright. If you're not sure, check with the Performing Right Society. Unless you really compose music, I'd forget about writing original comedy songs.

Poetry

Another way of breaking the standard pattern, of changing the pace of a show. Obviously, it's got to be amusing and it's not really enough for the performer to just stand there and read it. I know Pam Ayres does that, but she's unique. If you write a poem, you should dress it up somehow. Perhaps illustrate it with appropriate 'slides', or stock film, or even specially shot film. Johnnie and I once wrote half a dozen longish poems for a sketch series we did. I can't resist giving you one. Let me set the scene.

A wooden lectern set against a panelled wall. The 'reader' is introduced by a very serious voice-over. 'Ladies and gentlemen, recently there has been a revival of apathy in the works of the little-known Victorian poet, Thespian Mungo. Tonight we are privileged to hear a reading of one of his poems entitled "Dan, Dan, The Highwayman", with gestures.'

Our reader (Bernard Cribbins, actually) would enter to a hail of rotten fruit. He'd be dressed as a fastidious dandy of the period, complete with scented handkerchief. He'd read from a large old leather book on the lectern, ducking tomatoes and cabbage leaves between each and every verse.

Dan, Dan, the Highwayman

Now Dan he was a highwayman, and roamed both far and wide,
And took the gentry's valuables by force.
He spent days astride the saddle as he roamed the countryside,
Which was odd, because he hadn't got a horse.

He cut a dashing figure with his new three-cornered hat,
Sitting firmly on his old three-cornered head.
He'd leap out in front of coaches, crying 'Halt!' and things like
    that.
But as a rule they ran him down instead.

If they stopped, he kissed the women, and not one of them
    refused.
The men he robbed, and didn't seem to care.
Though there was one foggy evening, when he got a bit
    confused,
But I think we'd better leave the matter there.

One night he held a coach up, not too far from where he dwelt,
And fired his pistol, calling for surrender.
Alas, he had forgotten it was still stuck down his belt.
It absolutely ruined his left suspender.

But then Dan met a tragedy. Hoist by his own petard.
Thought he needed further practice with his pistol.
Stuffed in the powder, and the ball, a little bit too hard,
And shot his ramrod half the way to Bristol.

His ghost still walks along those parts. 'Tis true, you need not
    mock.
He haunts along the M4 motorway,
Leaping out into the fast lane, with his pistols at half cock,
And getting flattened fifty times a day!

Oh, well. Maybe you had to *be* there. All I can tell you is that
we had several people write in, seriously asking where they could
buy a copy of Thespian Mungo's works! A small bonus on this
poetry routine . . . we got to throw the tomatoes. If Bernard ever
fluffed a line, we were allowed to hit him with one. I don't think
he ever did.

One final comment about any poetry items that you write:
make sure they rhyme. Robert Frost summed it up when he said,
'I'd as soon write free verse as play tennis with the net down.'

Another piece that I would call a novelty item was a one-man theatre, in which Tommy Cooper came on wearing a split costume. The right half was an immaculate German officer's uniform and the left half was a ragged, British prisoner of war outfit. A funny picture immediately, as he faced front and did the opening spiel, setting up the item.

> TOMMY. And now, one man theatre, in which I shall play four hundred different people. Luckily, three hundred and ninety-eight of them aren't in this scene. Only him . . . and him. (INDICATES HIS LEFT AND RIGHT.) Picture the scene . . . Germany, 1940. Or twenty to eight. Stalag Thirteen, a prisoner-of-war camp just outside Schlessen . . . Schlossee . . . schless . . . Berlin. The leader of the escape committee, Captain Charles Creamtea . . . (TURNS TO SHOW BRITISH SIDE ONLY.) See? He's one of the Devonshire Creamteas . . . and he's face to face with the brutal Kamp Kommandant . . . (TURNS SO GERMAN SIDE IS FACING AUDIENCE.) . . . Hans Neizen . . . holder of the Iron Boompsadaisy and bar.

> DURING THE FOLLOWING, TOMMY TURNS TO SHOW THE APPROPRIATE PROFILE FOR EACH SPEECH.

> TOMMY (GERMAN). Zo! Last night six hundred and seventy prisoners escaped. How do you account for zis, Captain?
>
> TOMMY (ENGLISH). You left the front gate open.
>
> TOMMY (GERMAN). Lies! Zey smuggled zemselves out in ze laundry baskets.
>
> TOMMY (BRITISH). How did you find out?
>
> TOMMY (GERMAN). Zey are on ze list. (PRODUCES LAUNDRY LIST.) Three shirts, two tea-towels, six hundred and seventy prisoners . . .

And so it went on, for about three pages, eventually finishing up with Tommy struggling with himself and shooting himself.

We did several of this sort of item, including the evil squire and the innocent maiden (same split costume device) and the clean-jawed lawman with the evil outlaw.

Other novelty items could perhaps include puppets, hand-held or operated by somebody out of sight. Or ventriloquist dummies or a live dog ... anything. You have to let your imagination roam free on this sort of stuff. If you can come up with the goods, you'll stand an excellent chance of selling it, simply because it *is* different.

I've left the two major items in any sketch show until last, mainly because I think they deserve a little more space. First let's take a look at those electronic cartoons, the 'quickies'.

18 : Quickies

'Quickies', as their name suggests, are very short pieces of material, sometimes entirely visual, sometimes verbal, sometimes both. A typical half-hour sketch show would contain up to half a dozen of them. They fall into three main categories.

In-studio quickies

These are recorded in the studio, using simple sets most of the time. They're almost always pre-recorded without an audience and slotted into the show on the night. This is done to save time. If it takes twenty minutes to change into a monk's outfit and the piece lasts fifteen seconds, you can see the problem. Sometimes they're a visual gag, such as this example. I'm laying it out the way I would on a proper script.

'FLOWERS QUICKIE' (1)

EXT: FLOWERSHOP: DAY:

OUTSIDE A FLORIST'S SHOP, A SIMPLE FLAT CONSISTING OF A WINDOW AND A DOOR.

IN THE WINDOW IS A LARGE SIGN THAT READS 'SAY IT WITH FLOWERS'.
THE DOOR OF THE SHOP OPENS. A MAN LOOKS OUT, A CUSTOMER. HE GLANCES

ABOUT, LEFT AND RIGHT,
THEN COMES OUT OF THE
SHOP.
HE IS CARRYING A WIRE
FRAME, COVERED IN SMALL
FLOWERS AND FERN, ETC. WE
REALISE THAT IT SPELLS OUT
THE PHRASE 'GET KNOTTED'
IN FLOWERS. HE LOOKS AT IT
HIMSELF, CHUCKLES GLEE-
FULLY AND GOES OFF DOWN
THE STREET, CLUTCHING IT.

The script layout for all quickies and sketches is exactly the same as the layout for any other show. Except that I'd put each quickie on a separate page to avoid confusion and I'd give each one a title for ease of reference. The number (1) after the title is because we did several quickies using the same set.

The other form of in-studio quickie is the verbal gag, such as this example.

'MAN AND HIS DOG QUICKIE'
(1)

INT: LOUNGE: DAY:

A MAN AND A DOG ARE SIT-
TING ON A SETTEE, WATCH-
ING TELEVISION. A WOMAN
IN AN APRON ENTERS,
SCOWLS AT THE SETTEE, DIS-
APPROVING.

WOMAN. Rex! How many times
have I told you? You're
not to get up on the fur-
niture! Get to your basket
in the kitchen immedi-
ately!

THE MAN GETS UP AND SLINKS OUT.

MAN.   Yes, my love.

THE WOMAN SITS ON THE SETTEE, LOOKING SATISFIED. SHE PETS THE DOG AFFEC-TIONATELY.

WOMAN. Coochie-coochie-coochie
. . .

Since time is at a premium, directors like to do more than one quickie in the same set. During the course of a sketch series you might see four or five quickies featuring two adjacent telephone boxes. The director will have shot all of them in one morning. He'll then drop them into the various shows when it suits him. He doesn't have to put them all in one show. And he doesn't have the expense of erecting the set week after week.

So, if you think of a good gag about two adjacent telephone boxes don't just send it in on its own. Write several quickies, utilising the one set. It'll save time and money all round.

The same thing applies to costumes. If you write something hilarious featuring three monks at dinner, don't leave it at the one gag. Write three or four more and send them all in together. Costume changes take time. Let's do a few more gags while our performers are dressed up. Common sense, again.

In-studio quickies often use some form of electronic trickery, either by editing the piece afterwards or using various technical devices at the time of recording. Your director can have a character, or a whole roomful of furniture, disappear in a twinkling and return again just as fast. Never mind how he does it. To him, it's easy. It's safe to say that if you can imagine it, it can almost certainly be done.

There's also a very useful method of mixing two completely different pictures together into one. It's called colour separation overlay at the BBC, or chromakey in ITV. For instance, if you fancy having a man in a bathtub singing the Hallelulah Chorus onstage at the Albert Hall, you can have it.

Your director won't have to rent the Albert Hall. He'll find a length of stock film of the interior, create an electronic 'hole' in it and fill the hole with a studio scene of your bathtub warbler. It does not always give a perfect result but it's very acceptable for a quickie.

Even more acceptable is a technique called 'scene-sync' by everybody. He'd use a small model of the Albert Hall, thus giving him 'depth'. He can track-in to the model with his camera 1. Using the colour separation overlay, camera 2 would add your singing bather. It's a better technique because the director has more control over both pictures.

Of course, all this technical wizardry takes careful setting up, which again eats into the recording time available. Still, it gives the series less of a 'studio-bound' feel. As does the second category of quickie, the filmed quickie.

Filmed quickies

Every sketch series will be allowed a certain amount of filming time as part of their budget. On a series of six shows, they might get six days of location filming – one day per show. Since the recording weeks are going to be hectic enough without taking a whole day off to do the filming, it'll usually be done a week or two before the first recording.

Filmed quickies give you a chance to write things that can't possibly be done in a studio. Things involving cars, boats, Buckminster Abbey ... anything you fancy. Usually, though, a director likes to keep within a few miles of the studio, otherwise he's wasting his filming time by travelling to the location.

The number of people involved in filming a simple quickie on location is mind-boggling. You'll often have thirty people behind the cameras, all essential and all needing to be regularly fed and watered. This means taking a mobile canteen, mobile changing-rooms, buses to travel in, tons of sound and recording equipment, props, make-up, the lot. And all to do about five minutes of edited film in one day, if you're lucky. Quite often you'll only have one camera and every shot will have to be separately set up. The long shot, the medium close-up and the close-up are the director's three basic shots. During these he can whip-pan, crab sideways or zoom in. He'll edit his various shots into a coherent sequence at a later date. None of this need worry you. You don't need to write camera directions on your script. In fact, it's wiser not to. So long as you clearly explain what you want in your writing, the director will work out the best way of doing it with the facilities he has.

Again, don't just write one film quickie. Time spent on location filming is even more valuable than studio time. If you're going to write a filmed 'Robin Hood' bit, exert yourself and write several.

As with studio quickies, the filmed ones fall into two sub-categories: those without dialogue and those with. Those without will often have music or sound effects dubbed on later.

On the following example of a filmed, visual quickie the exaggerated 'bonk!' of the mallet and the water splashes would be dubbed over some appropriate bouncy music before it was played back to an audience.

FISHING QUICKIE: (1) (TELE-CINE)

EXT: RIVERBANK: DAY:

A FISHERMAN SITS ON A LITTLE STOOL, FISHING INTO A RIVER. BESIDE HIM IS A LARGE MALLET.

HE SUDDENLY GETS A BITE AND STARTS TO REEL IT IN. IT TAKES AN ENORMOUS EFFORT.

WE REALISE WHY WHEN A FROGMAN STUMBLES OUT OF THE RIVER. THE HOOK IS CAUGHT IN HIS OXYGEN TANK.

HE WADES OUT OF THE WATER, COMES UP TO THE FISHERMAN AND GESTURES ANGRILY AT HIM.

THE FISHERMAN APPEARS TO BE APOLOGISING, UNTIL HE SUDDENLY SNATCHES UP THE MALLET AND BONKS THE FROGMAN OVER THE HEAD WITH IT.

AS THE FROGMAN'S EYES GLAZE AND HE STARTS TO TOTTER, WE SEE THAT THE FISHERMAN HAS A LARGE, SIX-FOOT-LONG SARDINE CAN ON THE BANK BESIDE HIM. IT'S OPEN, WITH A LARGE KEY IN THE LID.

THE FROGMAN FALLS INTO THE TIN, ALONGSIDE TWO OTHER FROGMEN ALREADY LYING THERE.

THE FISHERMAN SMILES AND PREPARES TO CAST HIS NEXT FLY.

You'll notice that in all these examples, I haven't used the name of any artiste. I haven't typed 'Harvey' or 'Pamela', it's always been 'Man' or 'Fisherman'. Obviously, it's more personal to type the name of the performer you're aiming at on the script, but suppose they don't want to buy it? You'd have to type the whole thing all over again to send it elsewhere. It's a decision you'll make yourself but I thought I'd mention it in passing.

You'll also notice the word 'Telecine' just after the title. This is to indicate that it's a non-studio quickie. Some people prefer to use the word 'Film'. Others type 'O.B.', which stands for 'Outside Broadcasting'. Any one will do.

The other sub-category of filmed quickies is the one with dialogue. A typical example is this one, one of half a dozen we did on the same simple theme. It was shot in a local gravel pit, rather than in the desert sands we mention.

'WATER, WATER QUICKIE'   (1)
(TELECINE)

EXT: THE DESERT: DAY:

AN UNSHAVEN MAN, IN TATTERED RAGS, IS CRAWLING OVER SAND DUNES, CROAKING FEEBLY.

MAN.   Water . . .! Water . . .!

HE PASSES ANOTHER MAN CRAWLING IN THE OPPOSITE DIRECTION. THIS SECOND MAN IS DRESSED IN TOP HAT AND TAILS, SLIGHTLY TATTERED BUT CLEARLY RECOGNISABLE.

2ND MAN. Champagne . . .! Champagne . . .!

THE FIRST MAN WATCHES THE SECOND MAN CRAWL OUT OF SIGHT, THEN LOOKS AT THE CAMERA.

MAN.	Bloody toff! (RE-SUMES HIS CRAWL-ING.) Water ...! Water ...!

Silly, I know, but it did get a laugh. That's the thing about an awful lot of quickies, both studio and film, you have to suspend your disbelief, use your imagination, be nonsensical, be illogical. The only question that need be asked is, 'Is it funny?' Quickies don't have to be real, or believable. They're electronic cartoons.

The third category is very close to a 'novelty item', except that you should do more than one of them, yet again. It's not quite a quickie and not quite a short sketch. If anything it's a longer quickie, so we'll include it in this section. When analysing humour, we're bound to get overlaps.

Longer quickies

Can be done in a studio, or on film. It will feature one performer, playing the same character in the same situation each week. I can best illustrate what I mean by giving you an example or three. This particular one started life as a single thought. What if we had a short-sighted lookout man in the crow's-nest of a sailing ship?

'CROW'S-NEST QUICKIE' (1)

INT: CROW'S-NEST: DAY:

THE CROW'S-NEST OF AN OLD-TIME SAILING SHIP. A SAILOR STANDS THERE, WEARING A STRIPED JERSEY, NECKERCHIEF, STOCKING CAP AND OLD-FASHIONED SPECTACLES. HE PEERS TO-WARDS AN UNSEEN HORIZON, THEN BECOMES EXCITED. HE POINTS OFF AND SHOUTS

DOWN TO THE UNSEEN CREW BELOW.

SAILOR. (EXCITED.) Land! 'Tis land! Land ho! 'Tis land, me hearties ... Land! Land! (LOOKS AGAIN.) No, wait a minute, I do tell a lie ... 'tis the great white whale! 'Tis Moby Dick hisself! The great white wha ... no, 'ang on ... it's land! Aye, land! Land ho, lads ... land. Land ... I think. No. No ... 'tis a pirate ship! Skull and crossbones! Heave to, lads! 'Tis a pirate ... a pirate! Avast down below ... no, wait. (LOOKS YET AGAIN.) 'Tis land! Aye, land! Land off the starboard bow ... land! Land! Or a man overboard ... or a raft ... or maybe a hurricane ... or ... No, no, 'tis land! Aye, me hearties! Land! Land!

(HE SNATCHES OFF HIS SPECTACLES IN TRIUMPH AND PEERS MYOPICALLY IN THE DIRECTION HE'S BEEN POINTING. HE LOOKS DOUBTFULLY AT HIS SPECTACLE LENSES.)

HE WIPES OFF A FEW SPECKS WITH HIS NECKERCHIEF,

PUTS THEM BACK ON, PEERS
OUT. HE SHUFFLES UNEASILY
AS HE REALISES THAT
THERE'S NOTHING AHEAD.
COUGHS, WHISTLES TUNE-
LESSLY, TAPS HIS FINGERS,
ETC.

That was the first one, which I must admit did tickle our col-
lective funnybone. The last thing a crew needs, up there on lookout, is someone who is indecisive. Obviously we couldn't do the
same gag all over again. Well, not quite.

'CROW'S-NEST QUICKIE' (2)

INT: CROW'S-NEST: DAY:

SAME SAILOR, UP IN THE
SAME CROW'S-NEST, LOOKING
OUT. HE SUDDENLY BECOMES
EXCITED. HE CALLS DOWN,
POINTING TO HIS LEFT.

SAILOR. Cap'n! 'Tis a pirate ship!
A pirate ship off the
port bow! (SUDDENLY
POINTS TO HIS
RIGHT.) And ... and a
school o' whales! A school
o' whales, cap'n! Off the
starboa ... (BEGINS TO
POINT IN VARIOUS
DIRECTIONS, IN-
CLUDING UP.) ... land!
'Tis land, lads! Land!
Whirlpool! Directly ahead,
me boyos! A whirlpoo ...
man overboard! There's a

man overboa ... sea mon-
ster! There be a sea mon-
ster! And ... and a hur-
rican! A twister, lads! Belay
the mainsail! A shoal o'
flyin' fish! Look at that,
Cap'n ... a shoal o' ...
fire! Fire on the quarter-
deck! (LOOKS DI-
RECTLY AT CAMERA.)
Cor, dear ... it's all go
... and we haven't even
left Portsmouth 'Arbour
yet!

You'll have to imagine the wild enthusiasm the character was capable of. Rowan Atkinson or John Cleese could easily have done the part. Actually, it was Bernard Cribbins.

'CROW'S-NEST QUICKIE' (3)

INT: CROW'S-NEST: DAY:

SAME SAILOR, UP IN THE
SAME CROW'S-NEST. HE'S
LEANING AGAINST THE
MAST, DOZING. HE WAKES
UP, YAWNS, GLANCES OFF
AND SUDDENLY BECOMES
ALARMED. CALLS DOWN,
AGITATED.

SAILOR. Avast! Avast below! 'Tis a
pirate ship! A pirate ship
on the port side! All hands
on deck! 'Tis a pirate ship!

PEERS OUT AGAIN. BEHIND
HIS BACK, UNSEEN BY HIM,

A BLACK-BEARDED PIRATE CLAMBERS UP INTO THE CROW'S NEST. EYEPATCH, HOOK, DAGGER BETWEEN TEETH, ETC.

SAILOR. 'Tis . . . aye . . . 'tis Blackbeard 'isself! 'Tis Blackbeard, lads! The scum o' the Spanish Main! Blackbeard! The foul-mouthed, evil scoundrel 'isself! The flinty-hearted, rotten thievin' butcher who'd cut your liver out soon as . . .

HE BECOMES AWARE OF THE PIRATE STANDING RIGHT BEHIND HIM.

SAILOR. . . . look . . . at . . . you . . . but who has a few good points that we ought to consider as well. (TUGS FORELOCK, LAUGHS FEEBLY AND PULLS HIS HAT OVER HIS EYES.) Ahahah . . . ahaulp!

One final comment. Some series use a lot of 'costume' or 'historical' gags, featuring cowboys, or knights and so on. Other series want all their quickies to be contemporary, set in the present day and only in the present day. Study your market before you send your material off. You could save yourself a lot of postage and some frustration.

19 - Sketches

The three basic rules for writing any sketch, whether it's short, long, studio, film, satirical, topical or just plain funny, are these:

1 Set it up.
2 Run it along.
3 Give it a twist.

That's all your really need to know about sketch writing, but I'm going to analyse it a lot more or I'll have a very short chapter.

Just like situation comedy, you'll start with a vague notion, a half idea, and you'll polish it up, making notes as you go along. 'Setting it up' is simply making sure that the audience knows what's happening, what the piece is going to be about, who the characters are. 'Running it along' is another way of saying that you should develop it, that your characters should begin to relate, to react to one another. And 'giving it a twist' indicates that you can't just leave it at that, you've got to have a sting in the tail, you've got to surprise your audience with an unexpected development. You need a 'tag'.

It's not essential but it's good to have a vague idea of what your tag will be before you start writing. Even on a sketch, it's no bad thing to have a story-line in your head, if not on paper. Occasionally you might even have an idea for a good tag and work backwards, doing the body of the sketch, then setting it up as quickly as you can. It happens that way sometimes.

And, as in quickies, you don't really have to worry about believability. A lot of sketches have one thing in common. They start off with a normal situation and introduce a 'mad element' (such as Marty Feldman) into it. It's this mad element set against normality that is the basis of many, many sketches.

Let's take an example. Here's the half notion. These days, what with kidney donors and heart transplants, the human body is full of bits and pieces that are useful to other people. What if someone who needed money was to try and sell off his bits and pieces before he was actually dead?

This will be a studio sketch, using just the one set. Better give it a title, for reference purposes. I'll lay it out as I would for a proper script.

'MEDICAL RESEARCH'

INT: HOSPITAL RECEPTION AREA: DAY:

A DOCTOR IN A WHITE COAT STANDS BY THE RECEPTION DESK, STUDYING A CLIPBOARD. A TANNOY LOUDSPEAKER IS ON THE WALL.

A MAN SHUFFLES THROUGH THE DOOR LEADING TO THE STREET. HE'S WEARING A LONGISH OVERCOAT, A FLAT CAP AND A MUFFLER. HE LOOKS SEEDY. HE GRASPS OUR DOCTOR BY THE ARM, ANCIENT MARINER FASHION.

MAN.   'Ere, 'ow much will you give me for my body?

DOCTOR. I beg your pardon?

MAN.   For medical research, mate. I'm offerin' bits of

meself for medical re-
search. If the price is
right.

DOCTOR. But most of the bits
you've got, you'll need.

MAN. Not after I've snuffed it.
You can have the lot,
then. Providin' I can 'ave
the money now, see. Fifty
pee for me coccyx, that's
fair, innit?

So far, so good. We've set it up. The audience knows what
we're on about. Let's run it along for a while. It's a bit of a one-
string fiddle, but it's outrageous enough for the single note not
to become repetitive. Well, not yet, anyway.

DOCTOR. I'm sure it is, but . . .

MAN. I've worked out what all
me bits and pieces are
worth. I've even tied a
price tag to some of 'em,
in case of accident.

DOCTOR. (GLANCING AT
WATCH.) Yes. Well, I
really . . .

MAN. (PATTING STOM-
ACH.) There's miles of
good intestines in there,
mate. Miles of 'em. If
you laid out my intestines
in a straight line from
'ere to Trafalgar Square,
d'you know what'd
happen?

DOCTOR. Er . . . no.

MAN. People would trip over
'em. So snap 'em up
while they're in good
nick. Miles of 'em. I can
belch at will, y'know.

DOCTOR. Very interesting, but . . .

THE TANNOY CLICKS INTO
LIFE.

TANNOY. (DISTORT, FEMALE.)
Will Doctor Farthingale,
the Head Surgeon, please
report to the operating
theatre immediately!

DOCTOR. (INDICATING TAN-
NOY.) Ah . . .

MAN. Never mind that! Look
. . . (HE PRODUCES A
GRUBBY BIT OF
PAPER.) 'Ere's a list I
made on the bus . . . with
all the prices marked.
That bit there . . . see . . .
it's reduced to clear, on
account of it's slightly
imperfect, due to an accident with a power tool.

DOCTOR. (LOOKS AT LIST,
DESPITE HIMSELF.)
Really? Yes . . .

MAN. Still worth 'avin',
though.

> DOCTOR. I'm sure it is, but ...
> (NOTICES AN ITEM.)
> One pound thirty? Item
> seven.

> MAN. Ah. That may seem a bit
> pricey on the surface but
> believe you me, it's worth
> every penny. Never been
> used. I keep myself to
> myself. And item eight
> ... A and B ... you'll
> 'ave to buy the pair. I'm
> not breakin' up a set.
> Kidneys don't like being
> separated.

THE TANNOY GOES AGAIN.

> TANNOY. (FEMALE, DISTORT.)
> Will Doctor Farthingale,
> the Head Surgeon, please
> report to the operating
> theatre immediately!

This is the second time we've heard the tannoy. We hope the
audience will think we're doing it to increase the discomfiture of
our doctor. We're not. We're 'planting' our tag.

> DOCTOR. It's been very interesting
> but ...

> MAN. Me liver! That's worth
> 'arf a dollar, surely? You
> wouldn't even 'ave to
> pickle it in alcohol. I done
> that already. And there's
> piles o' bones in me, as
> well ...

DOCTOR. Perhaps the Battersea Dogs Home . . .

MAN. All right, then. Me brain. 'Ardly been used. Not to mention me skull . . . for the 'ospital players . . . 'Alas, poor Yorick' and all that . . .

DOCTOR. Now look, there's an emergency . . .

That's about it. That's all we're going to get out of this piece. The one note will get boring if we carry on much more. Let's get to our twist.

TANNOY. (FEMALE, DISTORT.) Will Doctor Farthingale . . .

THE SEEDY LITTLE MAN SNATCHES OFF HIS CLOTH CAP AND BELABOURS THE TANNOY WITH IT.

MAN. Oh, for Gawd's sake! (HE QUICKLY TAKES OFF HIS LONG OVER-COAT AND HIS MUF-FLER. HE THRUSTS THEM INTO THE DOCTOR'S ARMS. UNDERNEATH HE'S WEARING A WHITE SURGEON'S SMOCK, WITH A SURGICAL MASK AROUND HIS NECK.) They never give

you a minute's peace!
(TO TANNOY.) I'm
coming, I'm coming!

HE SLIPS THE
SURGICAL MASK UP
OVER HIS CHIN AND
MOUTH AND GOES
OFF, MUTTERING,
LEAVING THE
DOCTOR STANDING
THERE, HOLDING
HIS COAT, ETC. THE
DOCTOR LOOKS
LONG-SUFFERING.

I'm not saying it's a brilliant sketch. I know it's not, but it did work. It lasted about two minutes and thirty seconds, including the studio audience laughter, so it had the merit of being short. I suspect that some of the audience saw the tag coming, but most of them didn't. They hardly had time. It's getting a lot harder to mislead your audience, especially the ones at home. They've seen so much sketch comedy, they're getting to know the patterns. In other words, don't underestimate them. These days they're pretty aware.

It's worth mentioning the dropped g's and h's. It's a good idea to suggest character by writing the occasional piece of phonetic spelling, or dropping in a colloquialism. Your characters, like people, shouldn't talk formally or in a stilted form of speech. People, unless they're being emphatic, do not say 'I do not', they say 'I don't'. You should reflect this natural rhythm in your writing, without overdoing it. To attempt a proper phonetic spelling of, say, a Glaswegian drunk, would defeat your purpose, since it'd look like a foreign language.

As I said, an enormous number of sketches are based on this 'mad element' principle. 'Python', 'Marty Feldman', 'The Two Ronnies' and 'Not . . .' all rely, or relied, on it very heavily. On most shows, the vast majority of unsolicited pieces will use this device, knowingly or unknowingly.

That's an excellent reason for you to try another approach. There are other approaches to sketches, done in studio, which are less easily defined, but I'll try.

The basis of many sketches is the sheer outrageousness of the created situation. The set-up is breathtakingly unlikely, but there it is, right in front of your audience's eyes. How the characters cope with that situation, whatever it is, will be where the comedy comes from. As in sitcom, the relationships between the characters is very important. You have to make it clear where they stand in relation to each other. Unlike sitcom, you don't have to sustain an unlikely premise for half an hour. It's a short sprint, rather than a marathon. Your audience will happily suspend their disbelief for three or four minutes, especially if they're laughing.

When you think about it, we laugh out loud because we're surprised. The unexpected verbal comeback, the sudden visual, the unlikely reaction, all jolt us into showing our appreciation by laughing. We occasionally show our appreciation even more by breaking into spontaneous applause.

So let's try to create a situation that's funny, rather than rely on introducing a 'mad element' and depending on that to get our laughs. And while we're about it, let's try to do some visual humour. 'The Medical Research' piece, apart from the tag, could have been done on radio.

'THE DENTIST'

INT: DENTIST'S SURGERY: DAY:

DENTIST'S CHAIR IN THE CENTRE OF THE ROOM, WITH ALL THE USUAL EQUIPMENT. AN ANGLEPOISE LAMP NEXT TO IT.

SMITH, A MIDDLE-AGED MAN IN A WHITE COAT, IS POTTERING ABOUT, LOOKING FOR HIS SPECTACLES. HE'S

OBVIOUSLY VERY, VERY SHORT-SIGHTED.

THERE'S A LARGE MIRROR ON ONE WALL. A DOOR LEADS TO AN OUTER WAITING-ROOM.

SMITH. (TO SELF.) I'm sure I put them down somewhere ... (FUMBLING ABOUT, HE ACCIDENTALLY PRESSES A BELLPUSH. A LOUD BUZZ COMES FROM THE OUTER WAITING-ROOM. HE IGNORES IT AND CARRIES ON LOOK- ING.) They must be here ...

THE DOOR TO THE WAITING-ROOM OPENS AND A MAN COMES IN. HE IS OBVIOUSLY IN PAIN. HE CARRIES AN OVERCOAT OVER HIS ARM.

MAN. (TO SMITH.) Good after- noon. I'm not one of your regular patients but ... (A TWINGE.) Oooh! (SITS IN THE CHAIR AND RESTS HIS HEAD ON THE HEADREST.)

SMITH. Can you see a pair of spec- tacles about? I'm as blind as a bat without them.

MAN. (ALARMED.) What? (STARTS TO RISE.) Oh, I think I'll ...

And that's our set-up. It's been done very quickly because it isn't funny. The first laugh will come on the patient's obvious alarm at the information he, and the audience, has just been given. Let's run it along.

SMITH. (PUSHES HIM BACK INTO THE CHAIR.) Oh, never mind. I'll have to manage without. Keeping talking, I'll find your mouth from that.

MAN. Look, if you can't see what you're doing . . . I mean, these drills . . . they're quite tricky if . . . (HE TURNS HIS HEAD, LOOK-ING FEARFULLY AT THE DRILLS. SMITH HOLDS HIS HEAD STEADY AND PEERS INTENTLY INTO HIS EAR, WHICH IS ABOUT WHERE HIS MOUTH SHOULD BE.)

SMITH. Open wide . . . wider. Good God! You've got no teeth left at all!

MAN. That's my ear!

SMITH. Is it? Then where's your mouth? (GROPES OVER THE PATIENT'S FACE.) Is that your mouth? Is it? (THE PATIENT MUMBLES, BECAUSE

SMITH HAS HIS HAND IN HIS MOUTH.) Yes, yes, it is. Now we're getting somewhere. (TURNS AWAY AND GROPES FOR A DENTAL SPATULA.) Put your tongue out. (HE FINDS A SPATULA, REMOVES HIS HAND AND TURNS BACK TO THE PATIENT. PICKS UP PATIENT'S TIE WITH THE SPATULA, PEERS AT IT.) Tongue out . . . right. My word! It's green, with blue spots on it!

MAN.   That's my tie!

SMITH.   What's your tie doing, hanging out of your mouth? (FINDS MOUTH AGAIN, PEERS INTO IT.) Ah! Don't move! I've spotted the trouble. Let's have a little light on the subject. (GROPES AT A SWITCH AND TURNS ON AN ELECTRIC FAN.) That's better. Now, you'll need an injection . . . (GROPES IN TRAY, FINDS A BALLPOINT PEN, HOLDS IT UP LIKE A HYPODERMIC AND CLICKS THE

RETRACTOR.) Hold still ... (GOES TO GIVE INJECTION.)

Every single one of these fairly simple visuals will be getting a good reaction from our audience. I have a theory that there's a tinge of relief in the laughter. They're glad it's not them in the chair. The problem that the performer will have is that his words will be getting drowned in the laughter. He'll have to plough through it or the sketch will play too slowly.

MAN. (CRANING AWAY.) I'd ... I'd ... I'd rather have gas.

SMITH. Oh, very well. (GROPES AROUND THE CHAIR, FINDS THE ANGLE-POISE LAMP AND PLACES THE BOWL OF THE LAMP OVER THE PATIENT'S NOSE AND MOUTH.) If you insist ... there. (THE MAN MUMBLES PROTESTS.) Don't fight it ... relax ... relax. (HE PICKS UP THE SLEEVE OF THE PATIENT'S OVER-COAT, WHICH IS HANGING OVER THE ARM OF THE CHAIR. HE DANGLES THE SLEEVE.) That's the way. Nice and loose ... relax ... relax. Now then ... (HE REMOVES THE ANGLE

LAMP. THE PATIENT SITS, POP-EYED WITH FEAR, THE LAMP BULB FIRMLY STUCK IN HIS MOUTH.) We'll soon have the little fellow out. (GRASPS THE METAL PART OF THE BULB WITH FORCEPS, SQUINTING AT IT.) It's the one with the gold filling, isn't it? (A TUG, THE BULB POPS OUT. SMITH HOLDS IT UP IN THE FORCEPS AND PEERS AT IT.) Good heavens, that's a whopper! (THE PATIENT GIBBERS. SMITH HANDS HIM A SMALL VASE WITH A POSY OF FLOWERS IN IT.) Rinse . . . rinse!

THE MAN DOES SO, CHOKING ON THE FLOWERS.

SMITH. Now, isn't that better? Hmmm?

MAN. (A WRECK AND STILL IN AGONY.) Yes! Yes! (A TWINGE.) Oooh! Much better! Much better! Oooh!

SMITH. That'll be ten guineas. Pay the receptionist.

We've run it along as far as we can. I reckon we've had fourteen good laughs from our audience. Let's get out while the going's good. Let's give it the twist.

MAN. (EXITS QUICKLY.) Ten guineas . . . yes. Thank you, thank you.

ON HIS WAY OUT, HE CROSSES THE RECEPTIONIST, A GIRL IN A WHITE OVERALL. SHE'S JUST COMING IN FROM THE WAITING-ROOM. SHE LOOKS AT SMITH, SURPRISED.

RECEPTIONIST. (TO SMITH.) Excuse me. What exactly are you doing in here?

SMITH. I'm the dentist. (HE SUDDEN-LY FINDS HIS SPECTACLES LYING ON THE FILING CABINET.) Ah!

RECEPTIONIST. No, you're not. You're the window cleaner! (SHE PICKS UP A BUCKET AND WASH-LEATHER WHICH WERE BESIDE THE FILING CABI-NET, HANDS THEM TO SMITH.)

SMITH PUTS ON HIS SPEC-
TACLES AND PEERS INTO THE
MIRROR AT HIMSELF.

SMITH.   Good heavens! So
                I am! Terribly
                sorry . . .

AND HE CARRIES ON WASH-
ING THE WINDOWS, LOOKING
SLIGHTLY   PUZZLED,   BUT
WHISTLING.

All right, I cheated a little. We stuck a 'mad element' in at the
very end, just to give ourselves a reasonable tag. It's allowed. But
the main part of the sketch was about two characters coping with
the situation they found themselves in. It was a different approach from the other piece. You'll notice that in both examples
the 'set up' was done as quickly as possible. If you have to take a
couple of pages to set up any sketch, you're trying to be too
clever or the situation is just too complicated. Again, in both
cases, the pace of the piece was set by one of the characters and
the other one just reacted.

Let's get ambitious. Let's try a piece with three characters.
This time we'll have two of our characters reacting to the situation. The comedy will come from their rational discussion of a
problem, their attempt to be normal in the face of the abnormal.
In this piece, the set up will be a little slower but hopefully the
silliness of the situation will sustain the audience interest. They'll
be intrigued.

'THE ESKIMO'

INT: DINING-ROOM: NIGHT:

AN   UPPER-CLASS   DINING-
ROOM.   SILVER   CUTLERY,
GLEAMING   CRYSTAL,   NAP-

KINS, CANDLES, ETC. THREE PEOPLE ARE SEATED AT THE TABLE. LORD CRAYFORD, A DISTINGUISHED-LOOKING MAN IN A DINNER-JACKET. HIS WIFE, LADY CRAYFORD, DRESSED WITH EQUAL ELEGANCE. THERE ARE PHOTOGRAPHS ON THE WALL OF AN ARTIC EXPEDITION TEAM, POLAR BEARS, HUSKIES AND SLED, ETC.

ALSO SEATED AT THE TABLE, LOOKING TOTALLY OUT OF PLACE, IS AN ESKIMO. HE'S DRESSED FROM HEAD TO TOE IN GREASY FUR AND HE'S CLUTCHING AN HARPOON IN ONE HAND. WITH THE OTHER HAND HE'S STABBING AT HIS FOOD WITH A KNIFE.

HE'S EATING NOISILY AND CARRIES ON DOING SO ALL THE TIME. HIS TABLE MANNERS ARE ATROCIOUS.

IT'S NEAR THE END OF THE MEAL.

LORD C. (TO WIFE.) A little more brandy, m'dear? (SHE SHAKES HER HEAD, TIGHT-LIPPED.) (TO ESKIMO.) A little more whale oil? (THE ESKIMO NODS AND GRUNTS. LORD C.

POURS HIM SOME. TURNS TO WIFE.) It was quite a surprise, finding old Chingachook on the doorstep this morning.

LADY C. (COOL.) Yes. Where did you say he came from?

LORD C. The Arctic. Met him on m'last expedition. (TO ESKIMO.) Walrus blubber to your liking? (ESKIMO GRUNTS APPROVAL.) He put us up in his igloo. Shared everything with us. Didn't you?

THE ESKIMO NODS, GRUNTS AND MAKES A RUDE SEXUAL GESTURE.

LADY C. Everything?

LORD C. Yes. Very hospitable people, the eskimos. (CHUCKLES NERVOUSLY.) D'you know, he even offered me his wife.

LADY C. Oh?

LORD C. (UNEASY.) Yes. And . . . I've been meaning to tell you this, Penelope . . . it's considered very rude to refuse.

LADY C. Charles! You don't mean you . . .?

LORD C. I'm afraid I did. Only for the one night, mind.

LADY C. But the Arctic nights are six months long!

LORD C. Ah, yes. You'd remembered that.

ESKIMO. (GIBBERISH, INDICATING LADY C. HUNGRILY, THEN INDICATING HIMSELF.)

LORD C. (TO ESKIMO.) Yes, I'm trying to explain that to her *now*.

Here's where our audience begins to realise the situation. They're ahead of us and they're pleased with themselves. They can see what's coming. The eskimo wants reciprocal arrangements. It's been a longish set up, as I said, but there have been laughs along the way. Let's run it along.

LORD C. (TO WIFE.) The thing is, when they go visiting anywhere . . . say, here, for instance . . . they expect equal hospitality.

LADY C. Well, naturally, they . . . (TAKE) Charles! You're not suggesting . . .?

LORD C. Exactly. Would you like some more brandy now?

ESKIMO. (MORE GIBBERISH AS HE EYES LADY C. AND MAKES SUG- GESTIVE GESTURES.)

LORD C. (TO ESKIMO.) Yes. Quite. Quite. With scat- tered showers to the north-east, I believe ... (TO WIFE.) The point is, Penelope, I gave him to understand that if he ever came over here, I ... well, you and he ... would ... you're not making this any easier for me, are you?

LADY C. Charles, this is the fourth eskimo this year!

LORD C. I know. I'm a very grega- rious person when I'm exploring.

LADY C. I refuse to allow this ... man ... anywhere near my boudoir!

LORD C. Of course, m'dear, wouldn't dream of it. I was thinking more of ... in the refrigerator ... make him feel at home.

ESKIMO. (GIBBERISH.)

LORD C. What? Oh, the hole in the ice? Straight down the pas- sage, second on the left.

THE ESKIMO STANDS AND CLUMPS TO THE DOOR. WE SEE HE'S WEARING SNOW-SHOES. HE EXITS.

LADY C. It's absolutely out of the question, Charles. You'll have to send him away.

LORD C. It's a matter of honour, dammit! If the truth is known, he's not very keen, either. I mean, to him, you're ugly.

LADY C. What?

LORD C. Well, look at you. No rancid whale oil in your hair ... no fishbone through your nose ... God, I don't know what I ever saw in you myself!

LADY C. You beast!

LORD C. Besides which, he thinks you're skinny.

LADY C. Does he? Well, you tell him that there may not be much of me, but what there is has been to Roe-dean.

LORD C. It's all the same in the dark.

LADY C. What is?

LORD C. I don't know. It's an old

eskimo saying. They have a lot of dark in the Arctic.

THE DOOR OPENS AND THE ESKIMO RETURNS. HE POINTS BACK OUT OF THE ROOM.

LORD C. Can't you? Oh, never mind. The butler will do it for you. (TO WIFE.) He's worried about his huskies.

LADY C. Is he? Dammit, Charles, it's so cold-blooded. A woman needs to be wooed ... given little presents ...

THE ESKIMO SOLEMNLY PRODUCES A LARGE WET FISH AND HANDS IT TO LADY C. HE MUTTERS GENTLE GIBBERISH. SHE LOOKS AT IT WITH DISTASTE, HANDS IT TO HER HUSBAND.

LADY C. Eeeeeugh!

LORD C. *Noblesse oblige*, old girl.

LADY C. (RELUCTANT.) Oh, very well. Just this once, Charles. I'll do it.

LORD C. (IMPRESSED.) You're a brick, Penelope. A true blue brick. (HE EXITS, HAND TO HEAD.)

So the sketch was really all about the argument between the two main characters: whether or not she should oblige her husband by sleeping with the eskimo. There have been gags along the way, as the argument developed, but her reluctance to do what he wants has been the main basis of the sketch. On to our tag.

> LADY C. AND THE ESKIMO STARE AT EACH OTHER FOR A MOMENT. THEN THE ESKIMO THROWS BACK HIS FUR HOOD. HE'S A FAIR-HAIRED YOUNG ENGLISHMAN. THEY MELT INTO EACH OTHER'S ARMS.

> LADY C. (WITH PASSION.) Rodney!

> ESKIMO. (PERFECT ENGLISH.) Penelope! We can't go on meeting like this!

One of the more traditional twists. He's not what the audience thought he was. But it worked, and we had a lot of fun getting to it. I can excuse a somewhat weak tag if the sketch itself is funny.

So, what, if anything, can we learn from the examples we've just read? First, that the three basic rules *do* work. Second, that we don't need to use a specific performer's name on our script. Third, that both the set up and the tag should be as crisp as possible. Fourth, that the main body of the sketch should have visual as well as verbal gags. Fifth, that you can digress from the main line of the comedy and come back to it, if the premise is strong enough. And sixth, that anything goes. When you're writing sketches you can let your imagination run riot. The initial premise only needs to be sustained for that short sprint.

Because sketches are over with so quickly, you'll find that most of the ones you write will have very few characters in them. Two, three, maybe four. You simply haven't got time to introduce and develop any more than that. The team shows, such as 'Python' and 'Not . . .', only have a handful of performers, anyway. They manage very nicely, occasionally bringing in a guest or a few extras. Even Benny Hill (who writes all his own stuff. Forget it) has his regular little gang of performers who appear in most of his shows. As do Russ Abbot and Dave Allen . . .

Incidentally, there's a second good reason for not typing the names of specific performers on your scripts. Your director may disagree that Rowan, for instance, should play the part of Lord Crayford. He may think he'd get more laughs if he played the eskimo. If you haven't been specific, he'll have no mental adjustment to make.

So far we've been dealing with relatively straightforward sketches, set in the present day and using standard sets. There are other approaches. Let's look at them.

(20) More about sketches

It's easy to fall into the trap of thinking that studio sketches have to take place in a familiar setting, such as a dental surgery or a dining-room. Not so. Thanks mainly to television itself, we've all become familiar with such exotic locations as nunneries, western streets, Parliament and the television studios themselves. We may never have actually been to any of them but we recognise them instantly when we see them on the screen. It's the same with characters. I've never met an eskimo but I knew what they looked like.

We're limited only by our own imagination. So forget the standard three walls and some furniture, forget the familiar and consider a few different approaches. They're still sketches but they're a little different from the norm. I won't give you any long, complete examples . . . it's about time you did some work. I'll just set them up and, if you're in the mood, you can take it from there.

The solo piece
A close cousin to the 'novelty item', mentioned before. It's simply a person lecturing the audience, talking directly to camera. If you want to, you can indicate that you need a short musical introduction and a (preferably humorous) caption to lead into the piece. This suggests it's a television programme inside a television programme. That's OK. Television feeds off itself a lot, as with the pseudo news items.

'DO IT YOURSELF"

INT: STUDIO: DAY:

SUITABLE MUSIC OVER THE CAPTION, 'DO IT YOURSELF WITH HAROLD HELPING'.

MUSIC OUT, LOSE CAPTION.

FADE UP TO REVEAL THAT WE'RE IN THE CORNER OF A WORKSHOP. HAROLD STANDS AT THE WORK-BENCH. OVERALLS, CHECK SHIRT. EVERY FINGER HAS A BANDAGE OR A STICKING PLASTER ON IT. THE WORKBENCH CONTAINS SAWS, DRILL, WOOD SHAVINGS, ETC.

HAROLD. Good afternoon. Last week I showed you how to make matchsticks out of a model of London Bridge. Today, I'd like to introduce you to yew. I love yew . . . I don't know how you feel about me . . . (HE SNICKERS AT HIS LITTLE JOKE, THEN CLEARS HIS THROAT.) . . . no, seriously, haha . . . it's a type of wood. (HOLDS UP A LENGTH OF WOOD, WINCING WITH THE PAIN OF HIS FINGERS.) Wood. Now,

> like plastic, it can be
> drilled and sawn, but
> it's more expensive. It
> doesn't grow on trees . . .

You get the idea. Harold will go on to give a dreadfully incompetent lecture, stuffed with gags and visuals, probably paid off with him hammering away at something and shouting, 'Oh, do it yourself!' as we fade out and bring up the music. You can use this approach with a wide variety of subjects, 'Now We're Cooking', 'Medical Matters', 'Painting by Numbers' and so on. If you do a piece that works, you might find yourself with a regular running character. But you must give him some character. He should be bad tempered, or incompetent, or accident-prone, or supercilious. Something for the performer to play with.

Alternatively, you don't have to pretend it's a television programme. You can go straight into a solo piece without any introduction. Your director will cut from whatever the last item was – or he'll fade to black for a second, then fade up again – to find your character mounting the pulpit steps.

'CHURCH APPEAL'

INT: CHURCH PULPIT: DAY:

A CLERGYMAN, IN FULL SUR-
PLICE, IS MOUNTING THE
STEPS TO THE PULPIT. ORGAN
MUSIC. FADE MUSIC DOWN AS
HE FACES THE UNSEEN CON-
GREGATION.

VICAR. Brethren, before the
sermon today, which is
entitled 'Sex and the suburban housewife', so it's
worth hanging on for . . . I'd
like to make a further appeal
. . . (A DRIBBLE OF RAIN

COMES FROM ABOVE, SPLASHING ON HIS HEAD. HE MOVES TO ONE SIDE WITH PRAC-TISED EASE. IT CON-TINUES TO DRIBBLE, INCREASING IN VOL-UME THROUGHOUT THE FOLLOWING.) ... ahem ... for contributions to the Church Restoration Fund. (LEANS FOR-WARD ON LECTERN. IT FALLS OFF.) So far this year we've only had nineteen pence ... and I would ask those of you who put but-tons in the box to use your own. Not tear them off the hassocks ... (POUNDS EDGE OF PULPIT. A CHUNK BREAKS OFF AND FALLS.)

That's the set up. He'll continue his appeal as the church falls apart around his ears and the rain deluges down. It won't be a long piece, maybe three pages. None of these solo efforts are worth much more. They're short, sweet and saleable.

The interview routine
Another example of television feeding off itself. You'll find that most sketch shows will have one of these pieces in them. It's usually set in a very simple stage set, similar to any chat show layout. The interviewer will be the straight man and his guest, or sometimes guests, will be the weirdo(s). Now and again it will be reversed, with the interviewer being a raving lunatic instead.

This example comes from a Tommy Cooper show, hence it was written specifically for him and his name is on the script.

'KARATE EXPERT'

INT: STUDIO: DAY:

TWO CHAIRS, A LOW TABLE IN BETWEEN, MICROPHONES. THE INTERVIEWER, SUAVE AND SOPHISTICATED, IS SITTING IN ONE CHAIR, TALKING DIRECTLY TO CAMERA.

INTERVIEWER. Hullo. Tonight we have with us in the studio one of the few holders of the black belt in all four Japanese fighting arts ... ju-jitsu, karate, origami and kung fu ... Mr Tomomoto Cooper!

APPLAUSE AS TOMMY SPRINGS INTO THE SET AND ADOPTS A FIGHTING POSE. HE'S DRESSED IN A JUDO COSTUME, WITH A BLACK BELT.

TOMMY. Banzai! (HE SITS.)

INTERVIEWER. Quite. Now, I understand that the degree of proficiency you hold is known as a Dan.

> TOMMY. Yes. I'm a second Dan.
>
> INTERVIEWER. So you're a Dan-Dan?
>
> TOMMY. Yes.
>
> INTERVIEWER. And what do you do for a living?
>
> TOMMY. A lot of people ask me that. I work in a laboratory.

And so it went on, with Tommy telling ridiculous tales of his life in Japan. Feed line, followed by gag, mostly. It's just another way of stringing connected gags together. But you still need to set it up, run it along and tag it.

The panel sketch

An extension of the above, equally incestuous. It's a take-off of one of those discussion programmes that feature on every channel. One chairman, two or three panel members. Subject for discussion: sex, religion, politics or anything vaguely topical that you fancy having a go at. Once again, you can make them all potty or well-meaning, depending on what your angle is. Often, though, it's better to keep an element of sanity in at least one character, if only to contrast with the others.

> 'TALKABOUT'
>
> INT: STUDIO: DAY:
>
> APPROPRIATE MUSIC OVER CAPTION: 'TALKABOUT.' MIX THROUGH CAPTION TO THREE SILHOUETTED FIGURES SITTING AT A LONG DESK OR PANEL.

LIGHTS UP, LOSE MUSIC AND
CAPTION. THE THREE FIG-
URES ARE: THE CHAIRMAN, A
BISHOP, A PSYCHIATRIST.

CHAIRMAN. (TO CAMERA.
CLIPPED, SIN-
CERE.) Good
evening. Tonight
we're going to
talk about one of
the great moral
dilemmas of our
time. (HE CON-
SULTS HIS
CLIPBOARD.)
'Pre-marital sox.'
(HE LOOKS
UNSURE AND
CHECKS HIS
CLIPBOARD
AGAIN.) Er . . .
yes. 'Pre-marital
sox.'

PSYCHIATRIST. (BAFFLED.)
Socks?

CHAIRMAN. (IGNORING
HIM.) We hope
to have a frank
and earnest dis-
cussion with Doc-
tor Frank Preedy,
a doctor, and
Bishop Ernest
Ludlow . . . uh

> ... a bishop.
> (TO BISHOP.)
> What does the
> Church have to
> say on this contro-
> versial subject?
>
> BISHOP.   (BAFFLED.)
>   Pre-marital socks?

And they went on to discuss the subject, gradually warming to their theme. 'Socks without love are a meaningless present.' Until, to their evident relief, the spelling error was corrected. To 'pre-marital sacks.'

These three examples of television sketches taking a poke at television itself involved none of the performers impersonating anybody. Their effectiveness depended on the audience being familiar with that particular type of programme. If anything, we were impersonating a programme. It's obviously better if the performer playing the chairman can imitate Robin Day, but it shouldn't be essential. The piece should work without that bonus.

The beauty of television is that it keeps setting itself up as a target for parody. It keeps coming up with personalities and programmes that you can take the mickey out of. Barbara Woodhouse, the Epilogue (known as the Godslot), commercials, newsreaders, David Bellamy, quiz shows ... the list is almost endless. The minute the general public becomes aware of a person or a programme, he, she or it is ripe for satirising.

And it's not just television. There's nothing showbusiness likes more than doing an occasional sketch about itself. Funnily enough, harking back to sitcoms, there's never been a really successful comedy series that had a showbusiness or a sporting background. Drama, yes, but not comedy. Even when the writer has known his subject well, the audience at home haven't wanted to watch, haven't been able to identify. I don't know why this is, but I do know that it isn't so with sketches.

The showbiz scene

Fertile ground for the writer. The audience seems to tickled to find itself (albeit briefly, maybe that's the answer) behind the scenes, or backstage. And it usually is the back of the stage in a theatre, rather than behind the scenes in a TV studio. It's possible, of course, to write a piece about the control box, or the make-up room, but somehow it seems too incestuous. You're going behind the scenes of what they're actually watching. You're breaking the spell, perhaps. So let's stick to the theatre. 'O.O.V.' means 'out of vision'.

'THE VENTRILOQUIST'

INT: DRESSING ROOM: NIGHT:

A SEEDY DRESSING ROOM, BARE BULBS AROUND THE MIRROR, A LARGE WICKER-WORK BASKET IN ONE CORNER.

A THEATRICAL POSTER ON THE WALL READS 'BIJOU THEATRE, TONIGHT, THE GREAT VENTRILLO, WITH LORD FRED.' AND HAS A HEAD AND SHOULDERS PHOTO-GRAPH OF THE MAN HIM-SELF.

'THE GREAT VENTRILLO', A MIDDLE-AGED MAN, IN A DINNER JACKET, IS PUTTING ON HIS MAKE-UP AT THE MIRROR. A KNOCK AT THE DOOR.

CALLBOY. (O.O.V.) Five minutes, Mr Ventrillo!

VENTRILLO. (CALLING.) Aye, righto! (HE LEANS ACROSS AND RAPS ON THE LID OF THE BASKET.) We're on in five minutes, son.

THE LID OF THE BASKET LIFTS AND HIS SON SITS UP. HIS SON IS ABOUT THIRTY, AND IS DRESSED AS 'LORD FRED', COMPLETE WITH MONOCLE AND FAR-TO-SMALL DINNER JACKET. DESIGNED FOR A TWELVE-YEAR-OLD, IT'S BURSTING AT THE SEAMS. HE'S IN MAKE-UP AND HIS HAIR IS PLASTERED DOWN AND PARTED IN THE MIDDLE. HE LOOKS RESENTFUL.

SON.   Yeah. Look, Dad, I've been meaning to talk to you about the act . . .

VENTRILLO. They still think you're a dummy, son. That's our dread and gutter.

SON.   They don't, Dad! Backstage they know! They've seen me goin' to the loo!

That's the set up. They continue to quarrel about exactly

whose act it is and the frustrations of being locked in a wicker basket for twenty-three hours a day. They never actually get to do the act onstage, but there's nothing to stop you writing a piece that's set onstage in the first place.

'MURDER MOST FOUL'

ESTABLISH AN AMATEURISH THEATRICAL POSTER READING 'THE LITTLEHAMPTON PLAYERS IN MURDER MOST FOUL'. MIX THROUGH TO:

INT: STAGE SET OF LIVING ROOM: NIGHT:

A MURDERER AND HIS POTENTIAL VICTIM STAND THEATRICALLY POSED, THE MURDERER POINTING A REVOLVER AT THE VICTIM.

WE HAVE COME IN AT THE CLIMAX OF THE PLAY.

MURDERER. You leave me no choice, Hargreaves. You know too much. I shall have to shoot you! (HE PULLS THE TRIGGER WITH A FLOURISH. CLICK! CLICK! CLICK! IT WON'T FIRE. HE IMPROVISES.) No, dammit! Shooting is too good for you . . . you shall die by the . . . uh

... (HE LOOKS ROUND, SEES A LARGE ORNAMENTAL SWORD IN A SCABBARD, HANGING ON THE WALL.) ... by the sword! Aye, the sword! (AND HE SNATCHES THE SWORD FROM THE SCABBARD. BUT ONLY THE HANDLE COMES AWAY, LEAVING THE BLADE BEHIND. HE DOESN'T NOTICE, BUT ADVANCES ON THE VICTIM WITH THE HANDLE POISED ABOVE HIS HEAD.) It's no use pleading for pity because ... (SEES THE VICTIM MAKING FURTIVE GESTURES TOWARDS THE SWORD HANDLE.) ... what? (HE REALISES, TOSSES THE HANDLE AWAY AND LOOKS ROUND, PANICKY.)

It carried on for a while, with the victim eventually reduced to making *sotto voce* suggestions about how he could be murdered. Eventually the curtain came down to scattered applause and the murderer, cursing the stage-manager, tried the gun one more time and shot himself.

This piece was based on a supposedly true story, which raises an interesting point. Is it ethical to take a story, or a joke, that you've heard, and build it up into a sketch? For myself, I don't see why not. One cannot copyright a joke and it's hardly plagiarism if you've embellished it and lengthened it into a workable piece. The danger is that, if it's a current gag going the rounds, other writers might have done the same. Or your director or script editor might have heard it. On balance, it's best avoided, but if it's too good to ignore, do it. You'll probably find that the original gag will finish up as only a tiny part of the sketch, anyway.

The drag sketch

Appeals to many directors and performers. I don't say that in any derogatory sense. They know the surprise value of a man suddenly appearing dressed as a woman, they understand the laughter it will provoke. You can use this device very successfully in a solo piece or you can work it into a sketch.

I don't mean the glossy drag act of a Barry Humphries or a Stanley Baxter. I mean the pantomime dame approach, perhaps best epitomised by Les Dawson when he does his housewife character. The hairier and more masculine, the better.

'CONVENT CONVICT'

INT: CONVENT OFFICE: DAY:

THE MOTHER SUPERIOR'S OFFICE IN A CONVENT. A PLAIN DESK, STAINED GLASS WINDOW, THREE HARD BACKED CHAIRS, ETC.

THE MOTHER SUPERIOR SITS

BEHIND THE DESK. IN FRONT OF THE DESK SITS A UNI-FORMED POLICE INSPECTOR. A KNOCK ON THE DOOR.

MOTHER S. Come in, Sister Agnes.

ENTER A NUN, IN FULL NUN'S HABIT. IT'S VERY OBVIOUSLY A MAN. HE'S GOT A MOUS-TACHE AND IS SMOKING A FAG END. HE'S STUDYING A FOLDED COPY OF A RACING GUIDE, MARKING HIS SELEC-TION WITH A STUB OF A PENCIL.

NUN. (TO HIMSELF, DEEP VOICE.) 'Flighty Sadie' ... seven to two on ... Lester Piggot up ... worth a oncer each way. (HE CROSSES THE ROOM AND SITS IN A VERY INELEGANT AND MASCULINE MANNER. LOOKS UP AND SEES THE INSPECTOR.) Cor, swipe me, it's the fuzz!

MOTHER S. This is Inspector Harcourt of the Yard. He suspects there may

be an imposter in our
little order, Sister
Agnes.

NUN.   (TO INSPECTOR.)
              Get away! Pull the
              other one, it's got
              bells on it.

INSPECTOR.   We recently found a
              convict's uniform
              buried nearby. It
              belonged to a certain
              'Fingers' Mulligan,
              who escaped from
              Dartmoor a year ago.

NUN.   (LIGHTING AN-
              OTHER FAG
              FROM HIS FIRST
              AND CROSSING
              HIS LEGS TO
              REVEAL THAT
              HE'S WEARING
              HEAVY BOOTS.)
              Yeah, well, if he
              was here, he'd have
              scarpered by now.
              Look, I gotta go,
              I'm in the middle of a
              quick pray, aren't I?

A nonsensical set up, possible only because our nun clearly
isn't what she's supposed to be. We carried on the discussion,
with the inspector becoming increasingly suspicious and eventually arresting the Mother Superior.

Obviously, you can't write this one, since we've already done
it, but you can start to think about using this approach in some

other sketch. You'll need an angle. Maybe the trumpet player who can only get a job in an all-girl band. Or the police sergeant, sending out his male constables in frocks to tempt the Hampstead molester. Or there may be something in the attitude of the Equal Opportunities Commission, which won't allow companies to advertise which sex they'd like their ladies lavatory attendant to be . . .

The drag sketch has a great tradition in comedy, going a lot further back than Old Mother Riley. Feydeau and Shakespeare didn't hesitate to have a man fling on a frock at the drop of a hat. Why should you?

The historical piece

Meaning anything that isn't set in the present day. All the sketches mentioned so far could be considered to be up to date, in the sense that they're in modern dress. As with quickies, some sketch series won't do anything else, but most of them are happy to occasionally dip back in time for their comedy (in more ways than one, sometimes).

So the historical (or maybe costume would be a better word) pieces are an important part of many shows. They add colour and variety and can often make pertinent comments about present-day attitudes and opinions. Whilst the performers are dressed as, say, Robin Hood and his merrie men, they'll usually talk in modern-day parlance. The dialogue is often paradoxical and riddled with *non sequiturs* but it all adds to the fun.

There's something intrinsically funny about Isaac Newton eating the apple as he's having the bump on his head seen to by a doctor. 'I can't overemphasise the gravity of this injury.' 'Gravity! That's it!' Followed by Isaac expounding his theory for the first time, to a skeptical physician who thinks the bump has addled his brains. Or two cavemen discovering fire and rain. 'Hey, this wet stuff makes that hot stuff sizzle!'

Opportunities abound! Historical figures such as Abraham Lincoln, Caxton, James Watt, Beethoven, Nelson, Drake, Sir Walter Raleigh and Uncle Tom Cobley can all be resurrected and featured in a sketch. As a general rule, if they object to being portrayed in a comedy show, then they're not dead yet.

Set designers love the challenge of this sort of piece. It gives them the chance to create something different in the studio, the hold of a sailing ship, a dungeon in the Tower of London, or perhaps a street in the old American West.

'THE DYING COWBOY'

INT: EXTERIOR   WESTERN STREET: DAY:

A STREET IN ANY WESTERN TOWN, CIRCA 1880. A FLAT OF THE   ENTRANCE   TO   THE 'BUCKET O' BLOOD SALOON'.

SOUNDS OF BREAKING FUR-NITURE   AND   MANY   GUN-SHOTS COME FROM INSIDE. THE SALOON DOORS SWING OPEN AND A DYING COWBOY, RIDDLED   WITH   BULLETS, TOTTERS OUT AND FALLS ACROSS THE SALOON STEPS.

HE'S CLOSELY FOLLOWED BY A SALOON GIRL, IN FISHNET TIGHTS AND FRILLY GAR-TERS. SHE'S A DIM BULB, BUT GOOD-LOOKING   WITH   IT. TEARFUL, SHE CRADLES THE COWBOY'S   HEAD   TO   HER BOSOM.

GIRL.   Jeb, Jeb! Oh, speak to
               me, Jeb!

COWBOY.   (WEAKLY.) I'm . . .
               I'm agoin', Maisie.

GIRL.　　Where are you goin', Jeb?

CREEP IN A VIOLIN VERSION OF 'HIGH NOON', LOUD ENOUGH TO HEAR, BUT NOT TOO OBTRUSIVE.

COWBOY.　Let me rephrase that. I'm dyin', Maisie. He beat me to the draw. Listen carefully . . . I want you to have m'gold mine, Maisie.

GIRL.　　Oh, I don't deserve it, Jeb.

COWBOY.　You do, Maisie.

GIRL.　　No, I don't, Jeb.

COWBOY.　You do.

GIRL.　　I don't.

COWBOY.　Look, Maisie, I haven't got a lot of time . . .

GIRL.　　You have, Jeb.

COWBOY.　Oh, fer gawd's sake . . .

He went on to explain the exact location of his goldmine to his dimwitted girlfriend. She didn't know any of the landmarks he was talking about. Eventually, in exasperation, he beckoned off-camera and two dinner-jacketed men with violins came on to the set. They continued to play 'High Noon' as he gave *them* his goldmine. Paradoxical, but anything goes when you're looking for a tag.

One final note about studio-based sketches. This handful of

basic examples can only give you a glimpse of what is possible. It's by no means a complete list. In analysing them, I've had to quote lines extensively because each and every sketch is different from any other. To continue to divide and sub-divide the categories would need a thick volume. And I think we'd find ourselves getting bogged down in theories and concepts when the real test of any sketch idea can be summed up by asking the same old question, 'Is it funny?' If you think it is, then set it up, roll it along and tag it.

There's one other type of sketch that we haven't yet considered, the 'film' piece. It's worth a short chapter of its own.

21 - Even more abunt sketches

The 'film' sketch is any piece that isn't recorded in the studio but instead is done out on location. As with the quickies, they're sometimes really done on film (either 16mm or 35mm) or they're sometimes done with television cameras. As TV cameras get lighter and smaller, the flexibility they offer to a director is beginning to equal that of a proper film camera. And, of course, there is no processing to wait for. The director gets an instant playback and can shoot it again if it wasn't right. Whether he uses film or tape makes no difference to you. You'll still write the same piece.

Everything that we talked about in the filmed quickies section applies equally well to these longer pieces. It's worth mentioning that you can start a sketch on film, continue it in studio, then finish it on film, if that's what's needed.

And, naturally, you can have sound when you're out filming, if there's dialogue in the piece. If it's purely visual, then the director won't bother taking a sound crew out with him. He'll dub on music and effects at a later date.

Weather and sound are frequently a problem when you're out on location. You're doing an historical piece. Henry the Eighth is just proclaiming his love for one of his wives. Suddenly a Boeing 707 screams across the sky. Retake. Reset the scene. The sun's gone in, it's started raining. You'll have to wait or the bits you've already filmed won't match. It's all time-consuming and rather boring for everybody concerned.

Despite these drawbacks, your director will sometimes go out and film a piece that could be done in the studio. He'll do this for one of three reasons. He's got some filming time left over and wants to use it up. He thinks it will look a lot better on film. Or he can't build the set in the studio because he hasn't got the space or the budget.

By and large, most of the longer filmed sketches are done with a minimum of sound or no sound at all. If you want rain or fog or snow or wind, various machines can provide them. Or it's possible for your director to add a 'fog loop', a 'snow loop' or a 'rain loop' when he's editing the piece later. This is simply a length of video tape which has nothing on it except rain falling or fog billowing. Your performer will do his bit on a bone-dry day, with his hair dampened and his coat collar turned up as though it were tiddling down. Later, the director will super-impose the rain loop over the picture and you've got what you want with a minimum of fuss or discomfort.

Whilst they can, and frequently do, record at night, they can also shoot in bright sunshine and, by cunning use of filters, the picture will come out as though it were midnight. It's called 'day for night' shooting.

As with the studio pieces, technical trickery can be used to vanish a bus, or a bus queue, then relocate them elsewhere. Stunt men or women can substitute for your fragile performers, if necessary. Most things are possible.

This example of a straightforward filmed piece would take up at least one whole day of any filming schedule, mainly because of the various locations.

'THE FLY' (FILM)

EXT: VARIOUS LOCATIONS: DAY:

START ON THE EXTERIOR OF AN ORDINARY SUBURBAN HOUSE. WE HEAR VOICES FROM INSIDE AND THE SOUND OF A NEWSPAPER THWACKING AGAINST A WALL.

MAN. (O.O.V.) I'll have it! (THWACK.) I will! Come here you little perisher! (THWACK.)

WOMAN. (O.O.V.) Oh, Arthur, it's only a fly!

MAN. (O.O.V.) It's been annoying me all day! (THWACK.) Where's it ...? It's flown out the letter box!

THE FRONT DOOR OPENS AND A MIDDLE-AGED MAN GLARES OUT WILDLY. HE'S IN SHIRT SLEEVES, BRACES AND SLIPPERS. HE CARRIES A ROLLED-UP NEWSPAPER. HE GLARES DOWN THE GARDEN PATH, THEN CHASES AFTER THE FLY, ALTERNATELY SWIPING AT THE AIR AND SPRAYING FROM A CAN OF FLY SPRAY.

MAN. There it is! Come here!

HE VAULTS OVER THE GARDEN GATE, CHASING AFTER THE FLY, DETERMINED. CREEP IN MUSIC 'THE FLIGHT OF THE BUMBLE BEE', MAKING IT LOUDER AND SOFTER WHERE APPROPRIATE. THE MAN AD-LIBS CRIES OF 'OI!' AND 'COME HERE!' ETC, FOR THE REST OF THE PIECE.

HE CHARGES DOWN THE STREET. A MAN IN A BOWLER HAT STANDS AT A BUS STOP, LIGHTING A CIGARETTE. C.U. A FLY ON HIS HAT. F.X. FLY BUZZ. OUR HERO CHARGES UP AND CIRCLES THE MAN, A WILD LOOK IN HIS EYE. THE MAN LOOKS WORRIED. EVENTUALLY OUR HERO SMASHES HIM OVER THE HEAD WITH HIS ROLLED-UP NEWSPAPER. F.X. FLY BUZZ. HE CHARGES AWAY, LEAVING THE BUS STOP MAN LOOKING STUNNED.

INTO A GARDEN. A WOMAN SITS IN A DECKCHAIR DOZING, HER MOUTH OPEN. OUR HERO CHARGES IN, LOOKS AROUND. HE PEERS DOWN HER MOUTH. A FLY BUZZ, WITH ECHO. HE WONDERS WHETHER TO SHOVE THE NEWSPAPER DOWN HER MOUTH, BUT EVENTUALLY SETTLES FOR A LONG SPRAY WITH HIS CANISTER.

ANOTHER FLY BUZZ. HIS EYES FOLLOW THE PATH OF THE UNSEEN FLY. HE CHASES AFTER IT.

THE WOMAN WAKES UP, STARTLED, LICKS HER LIPS. SHE SWALLOWS, THEN HER

EYES GLAZE OVER AND SHE
FALLS SIDEWAYS OFF HER
DECKCHAIR.

And so the piece went on, with our hero determined to catch
and kill the fly. We used several different locations and about a
dozen sight and sound gags, including him chasing the fly
through a car wash and a china shop. The sketch came full circle
when he finished up at his own front door again and his wife
casually squashed the fly herself. Our hero, enraged, began chasing her.

It's a simple but effective method of stringing together a
bunch of jokes. All you need is an imagination and a theme. It
doesn't have to be a chase. It could be a picnic or an outing to
the seaside. Any theme that will provide a continuous sequence
of linked gags.

The biggest problem with selling these filmed visual sketches
is that they don't look all that funny on paper. The director or
script editor has to use his imagination, has to see the dubbed,
edited, fully finished version in his mind's eye. You can help by
making sure that your script is readable. The description of each
gag should be as crisp as possible. Don't waste words. And lay
each gag out separately, as in this example. Don't run the whole
thing together, it's off-putting to the reader.

I think I'm beginning to repeat myself. Let's move on.

(22) Solo or duo?

We're heading towards the end of this longish lecture on comedy writing, and I feel I ought to pay an overdue acknowledgement to my long-time partner. Johnnie Mortimer and I wrote most of the pieces I've used to illustrate this book and I'm indebted to him for his permission to use them.

And while we're on the subject of partners, it's worth considering whether or not you might benefit from working with another writer, or forming a team. There are pros and cons, as you'd expect.

Some of the best sitcoms and sketch shows on television have been written by two people working in harness. I think I know why. It's because they strike sparks off each other. They get an immediate reaction from each other when they come up with an idea or a line of dialogue. And even when they're both feeling a little below par, they're still firing on the same number of cylinders that either one of them can produce on a normal day. The one thing that any comedy writer can't get enough of is encouragement. To come up with a funny line and have it instantly confirmed as a funny line is the most encouraging thing that can happen. And if a partner then tops it with an even funnier comeback, then you can get a lift that lasts a whole morning. The right partners enthuse each other.

There's also an element of 'showing off', of being on your toes to produce the best that you can. If you find yourself working with someone who isn't doing his fair share, you'll both know and it won't last long. Solo tennis might be a good game, but it never caught on. It takes two players to give most games the competitive edge that can bring out the best in both of them. If you belt the ball over the net and it doesn't often come back, you might as well be playing alone.

There's no known way of finding the right partner. In our case, we both used to play the guitar and thought we'd practice together. Unfortunately, he played classical style and I strummed. Once we'd mastered Lonnie Donegan's 'Air on a G string', there didn't seem much left to do. So we started writing comedy.

If you do find someone that you fancy writing with, it's rather difficult to do it long distance. He or she will have to live nearby, so that you can sit down and get on with it in some mutually compatible place. I don't think it can work if you do your bit then post it halfway across the country to get your partner's reaction. You lose most of the benefits of working with somebody else if you're not sharing an office. Or at least a desk. We started on a pull-down ironing board in a kitchen. Well, it was quiet and we could reach the coffee without stopping our scribbling.

The disadvantages of working as a writing team can easily be summed up. He takes half your money. He won't think of it in quite the same way. He may even consider that you're taking half of his, especially if you're the one who isn't lobbing the ball back quickly enough.

Writing partnerships, rather like a marriage, can grow. You should find yourself eventually writing to a standard that is higher than either of you can manage on your own. There's almost a third person to please, a sort of Marty Took or Frank Norden. Fortunately, he doesn't get any of the money, so you're no worse off.

If you've worked with a partner for a long period of time, you find yourself writing as though he was there, even if it's a solo effort. Very odd . . . something to do with habit, or an ingrained working pattern. Or possibly an attempt to reach this higher, third-person standard, on your own.

Of course, there have been just as many highly successful comedy shows written by solo writers. And they get to keep all of the money. They also don't have the frustration of coming up with an hilarious line, only to have it greeted with a blank expression or a mumbled 'Um . . . I'm not besotted with that . . .'.

In truth, most solo comedy writers do not work in a complete vacuum. They use friends or relatives as a sounding board. You have to be a little careful here. Auntie Hilda or Uncle Wilf (remember them?) will probably think it's marvellous that you can string two words together, let alone type a whole page of script. They'll recall you tap-dancing on a biscuit tin on your fourth birthday and think that you're a born entertainer anyway. In a word, they're biased.

And they're not really equipped to read a script and reconstitute the visual images that were in your head when you wrote it. That's the director's job. Actually, as a selling solo writer, you'll find that the good directors partly fulfil the role of a partner. And the script editor on a sketch series will do the same. They have to; it's part of their job to encourage their writers.

Even so, the solo writing of a script can be a lonely business. You're the only one turning your engine over and there will be days when you'll keep misfiring. The dreaded writer's block isn't too bad when there are two of you. When you're working on your own, it can seem insurmountable. If it's any consolation, I usually get it about every third line. All you can do is find your way round it, through it, under or over it. Press on with the piece, accepting the fact that you can return to that part later and polish it up. Don't let yourself be blocked for too long. When you do return, perhaps the following day, you'll frequently find that it's not the problem you thought it was. I'm a great believer in mulling things over, in letting the subconscious do a little of the work for me.

Whether you decide to work alone, or try writing with somebody else, is really down to your own individual temperament. You will have to subjugate some of your own personal style of writing if two of you are creating something together. But you'll also be learning, seeing another point of view, adapting to a different approach, tackling problems in a way you may not have considered if you were doing it alone. Maybe you'll be lucky enough to find the right writing partner, one you enjoy working with, one who pulls his weight, who complements you. And vice versa.

Let's face it, the worst that can happen is that you decide you've made a mistake. So you split. You're still better equipped to write on your own than you were before.

I can't deny that there is an enormous satisfaction in creating a whole show on your own, or writing a good sketch without anybody's help. At the same time, if it goes wrong, it's quite nice to have somebody to share the blame.

BBC Producer, eh? You fellers have turned down my last twenty-seven scripts . . .

23: Tidying up

I mentioned earlier that we'd take a look at ways of breaking into the market place, but I think I can sum it up in one word. Persistence. When it comes to selling sketches and quickies that's the one thing you can't have enough of.

Unlike situation comedies, where you can shoot off a fully finished script, the marketing of your sketches and quickies will be more of a buckshot pattern. You're going to spray 'em out in all directions, hoping you'll hit something. First, though, you'll have to sort out your targets.

Advance notice of what's coming up in the way of sketch shows is hard to come by, especially for a new writer. So you're going to have to turn into a detective. First things first, if you know anybody at all who works in television, whether it's a secretary or a doorman, use them. Ask them who's who in their company, find out what's being recorded, get some names. Contacts are the most useful source of information. A friend of a friend will do nicely.

Send out letters to every television company you can think of, asking what their current and future requirements might be. Take another look at chapter nine. Write to directors personally, asking if you can submit some of your material for their consideration. Accept the fact that you might get vague replies, or no replies at all. If you get a nugget of information, follow it up quickly. Send in several samples of your work. Be a nuisance, be persistent.

Read the *TV Times* and the *Radio Times* carefully. Check the names of the directors, producers, script editors. Find out which company they work for and send your material to them via that company. Keep your fingers crossed that they're still there.

Study the 'Television Today' section of *The Stage*. In fact, order it from your newsagent. Rummage through the television pages of the national newspapers and magazines. They frequently feature articles about, or interviews with, performers. The performer may have mentioned that he's doing a second series, or a first series of something in the not too distant future. Bingo! Send him some of your stuff. Spray it out. It's not going to sell to anyone if it's stuck in one of your desk drawers. You won't know the performer's address, so send it care of whatever TV company he's working for. All you're trying to do is to draw attention to yourself and your work. He won't mind at all. He'll be flattered.

If it's at all possible, attend some television show recordings. Write in to the ticket unit of whatever company is nearest to you, asking for tickets to any sketch or variety show. Don't specify, take pot luck. Try and get up to the bar afterwards. There's always a bar. The writers/performers/directors all like to relax after the recordings. Join them. If you're stopped by a uniformed commissionaire, bluff a little. 'I'm one of the writers . . .' isn't exactly a lie. Mingle. Listen, talk. Ask questions. I know it's nothing to do with writing; it's all to do with the other half of your job, selling the stuff.

Don't get discouraged. I know that's easy to say, but you have to accept the fact that rejection slips are part and parcel of any writer's life. I once papered a whole wall with them. Always make sure that you've got some material out, that tomorrow may bring the breakthrough. And while you're waiting, be writing something else.

Above all, make your writing a habit. Every successful television writer has made his work important to his feeling of wellbeing. If he takes a few days off, he feels guilty. So sit down and write something every single day, preferably about the same time. It doesn't matter whether it's early morning or late evening. Develop a regular pattern of work, be disciplined with yourself.

And that's about it. I'm not leaving you on your own. I hope this book will become a well-thumbed workmate. One final thing. Your determination to succeed is the most important thing you've got going for you. Don't lose it.

Good luck.

Useful addresses and books

Addresses

The Writers' Guild of Great Britain, 430 Edgware Road, London W2 1EH. Telephone (01) 723 8074. The writers' trade union. The Guild has negotiated minimum fee agreements for script-writers with the BBC and ITV companies.

Independent Broadcasting Authority, 70 Brompton Road, London SW3 1EY. Telephone (01) 584 7011. For names and addresses of ITV companies, see *Who Does What on ITV*.

BBC TV networks script submissions: send to the Head of TV Script Unit, BBC Television Centre, Wood Lane, London W12 7RJ. Will send information about current requirements.

BBC Radio submissions: send to the Script Editor, Light Entertainment (Radio), BBC, Broadcasting House, London W1A 1AA.

Channel 4, 60 Charlotte Street, London W1. Commissions programmes from independent producers. Send scripts to the Commissioning Editor Light Entertainment Department.

The Performing Right Society, 29–33 Berners Street, London W1P 4AA. Will give advice about copyright in songs and musical works.

Handbooks and directories

Writers' & Artists' Yearbook. Published annually by A. & C. Black. Available in libraries everywhere. Contains information and advice about how to sell your writing, whether for TV, radio, theatre or books, and about related subjects like literary agents, copyright and tax. Lists the addresses of all major markets for TV scripts both British and Commonwealth.

Television and Radio (formerly called *IBA Guide to Broadcasting*). All about independent broadcasting, including programming policies and names and addresses of ITV companies. Available from the IBA, 70 Brompton Road, London SW3 1EY.

Who Does What on ITV. Lists names and addresses of ITV companies. Free leaflet available from the IBA.

ILR: Who Does What. Lists names and addresses of independent radio companies. Free leaflet available from the IBA.

Writing for the BBC. All about what the BBC requires and what they pay freelance writers. Available from BBC Publications shops or PO Box 234, London SE1 3TH, or from larger bookshops and newsagents which stock BBC books.

BBC Handbook. The BBC's annual report all about its activities during the past year. Can be bought from BBC Publications, from large bookshops or newsagents, or borrowed from libraries.

Interesting reading

Bart Andrews and Brad Dunning, *The Worst TV Shows Ever* (E.P. Dutton, New York).

Desmond Davis, *The Grammar of Television Production* (revised by John Elliot), (Barrie & Rockcliff, London).

Marie Donaldson (ed.), *Anatomy of a Television Play: An Enquiry into the Production of Two Armchair Theatre Plays by John Russell Taylor* (Weidenfeld & Nicolson, London).

Marie Donaldson (ed.), *Both Sides of the Camera* (Weidenfeld & Nicolson, London).

Janet Dunbar, *Scriptwriting for Television* (Museum Press, London).

Stan Hayward, *Scriptwriting for Animation* (Butterworth, London).

Lewis Herman, *A Practical Manual of Screen Playwriting* (Forum Books, Cleveland and New York).

Robert Hewison, *Irreverence, Scurrility, Profanity, Vilification and Licentious Abuse: Monty Python: The Case Against* (Methuen, London).

Dorothy Hobson, *Crossroads: The Drama of a Soap Opera* (Methuen, London).

David Nathan, *The Laughtermakers* (Peter Owen, London).

Eric Paice, *The Way to Write for Television* (Elm Tree Books, London).

Robert J. Wade, *Staging TV Programmes and Commercials* (Chapman and Hall, London).

Roger Wilmut, *From Fringe to Flying Circus: Celebrating a Unique Generation of Comedy 1960–1980* (Methuen, London).